SEAN DUFFY

DOUG HARVEY
VERONICA FERNANDEZ

FRONT FORTY *PROFILES* SERIES
№ 2

FRONT FORTY PRESS / CHICAGO

Editor __________________ FRONT FORTY PRESS

Series Designer ________ CAITLIN BAULER

Copy Editor ____________ CHRISTINE DiTHOMAS

Harvey, Doug
Sean Duffy / Doug Harvey, Veronica Fernandez. -- Chicago, Ill.:
Front Forty Press, ©2011.
p.; cm.
(Front Forty Profiles Series ; No. 2)
ISBN: 978-0-615-40146-1
Includes index.
1. Duffy, Sean, 1966- 2. Artists--United States--Biography--21st
century. 3. Art, American--21st century. 4. Identity (Philosophical
concept) in art. I. Fernandez, Veronica (Veronica M.), 1978- II. Series.
N6537.D824 H37 2011
709.2--dc22 1105

Printed in Korea

www.front40press.com

FRONT FORTY PRESS

ESSAY

by DOUG HARVEY

PLATES

Q&A

with VERONICA FERNANDEZ

CATALOG

What Dreams May Come Again

SEAN DUFFY'S CONSUMER PARADISE

by

DOUG HARVEY

Sometimes when I'm looking at Sean Duffy's work, I get the weird feeling that I'm eavesdropping on somebody's near-death hallucination—or even their trip through the Bardos to whatever's beyond that great white light. It isn't that the sculptures, paintings, installations, etc., Duffy has created over the last two decades are morbid—or particularly spiritual.

But imagine you're walking through the mall and you start to notice that all the items on display are a little strange—a music store displays only a couple of old-school vinyl obscurities, in huge quantities. The furniture emporium contains weirdly mutated iconic modernist design at one end, and generic office decor repurposed into some kind of post-apocalyptic Zen garden at the other, with a bunch of weird-ass lamps made from castoff electric fans and plastic gas cans in between.

The home entertainment big box is chock-full of perversely customized equipment from that parallel universe where John Cage's multiple-turntable audio collage chance compositions topped the charts. And don't get me started on the AutoZone! The point is, everything is a little off, sometimes way, way off. But it isn't random—each distortion has the distinctive stamp of being related to a specific person, like in a Philip K. Dick story where supposedly benign fragments of objective reality start turning into explicit personal messages. Only the messages aren't for you. They're for Sean Duffy.

And they're from Sean Duffy. But are they the same guy? One of the most compelling aspects of Duffy's oeuvre is the fact that it straddles the two personae that every artist has to reconcile—the inward-looking, self-reflexive, isolated human consciousness that comes up with the goods and the outward-facing, collectively mediated social animal that puts them on display. And although this whole Personalized-Shopping-Mall-of-the-Damned scenario sounds a little solipsistic, anyone who's seen Duffy's work can attest to its genuine popular appeal.

This, strangely enough, is due in large part to the fact that it is Pop Art. Duffy's earliest solo shows in Los Angeles included re-creations of scenes from the original *Star Trek*, from pieced-together Day-Glo fun fur compressed onto a TV-shaped surface under clear upholstery vinyl, melding a personal and generational yearning for heroic male role models (however preposterous—sorry Bill) with a complex but highly palatable critical engagement with issues surrounding contemporary painting practice and visual culture in general.

With each of his subsequent bodies of work, Duffy has expanded the layers of cultural resonance available to the viewer, harnessing the visual vocabularies of subcultures from vinyl-fetishizing record collectors to holdout advocates of 1960s post-painterly abstraction, from the high-end clientele for mid-century modern furniture design to the down-and-dirty improvisations of stock car racing enthusiasts. And he mixes them up—creating, for example a mash-up of George Nelson's *Marshmallow Sofa* with the Mod-era target logo of The Who—itself a commercial appropriation of a then-cutting edge abstract painting motif common to Jasper Johns, Kenneth Noland, and others—or sewing a *Drunkard's Path* quilt (in itself a free-standing feminist critique of the supposed innovations of serial geometric abstractionists) out of T-shirt scraps left over from another art piece; the distinctive broken-curve pattern created with a vinyl record label acting as a stencil for KILZ spray-paint, a brand marketed for its capacity to eradicate graffiti.

To add to the confusion—and expand the potential points of audience engagement—Duffy's output regularly references work by other contemporary artists mining some of the same cultural veins, various trickle-down hobbyist incarnations of high design. I'm thinking particularly of his recent craft project reiterations of Buckminster Fuller's utopian geodesic architecture as decorative lamps (*dark wood lights*, 2010) and cocoon-like easy chairs (*Tunix of My Apathy I & II*, 2007), and earlier artifacts from his own oeuvre.

The accessibility of this fractal, rhizomatic network of popular visual associations is aided and abetted by Duffy's sense of humor, which combines absurdist dislocation with affectionate attention to anecdotal detail in equal measure, defusing both the exclusivity of the "high" cultural references and the classist stigma of the "low." This metaphorical spatial disorientation—the disruption of top-to-bottom rankings of aesthetic phenomena—is made literal in works like *The Grove* (2007)—Duffy's epic, touring spiderweb of interactive audio collage components, where the signal from each turntable station is dispersed among scores of dangling speakers.

This destabilization of symbolic and structural placeholders is reiterated in the temporal distortions of Duffy's multiple-tonearm and drastically variable-pitch turntables (his most recent extended Elvis' 4-minute 1968 recording of "A Little Less Conversation" to more than two hours of rumbling drone—in that John Cage dimension it's outsold Junkie XL's remix 33-1!) as well as in the artist's ongoing exploration of imperfect clones, analog distortion, and cover versions.

Probably the most evident manifestation of this disorderly impulse is in Duffy's indeterminate interactive strategies—perhaps most clearly articulated in *The Grove*, most rigorously in the potential permutations of grid compositions inherent to his record and magazine silkscreen display "paintings"—but nowhere more delightfully demonstrated than at his 2010 installation in the LA Municipal Art Gallery, where young children could be seen gleefully cranking the tiny musicbox mechanisms embedded in slablike fragments of a 1979 Mazda RX7 sportscar (noted for its incorporation of the Wankel rotary engine) to generate looping, overlapping renditions of Michel LeGrand's timeless classic "Windmills of Your Mind."

Such are the considerable lengths to which Sean Duffy manipulates the outer aspects of his work to invite the participation of his audience, and the result is a beautifully complex moiré of cultural referents. But we have momentarily lost sight of the fact that this is Sean Duffy's quasi near-death experience we are peeping in on, and that each of these clusters of signifiers is loaded with a specific self-reflexive autobiographical charge. From the actual-size replication of his father's zebra-striped 1964 Toyota Land Cruiser (*Car 23*, 2008-2010) to the complex mosaic self-portraiture of his modified record sleeve installation/sculpture *Group Show* (2006), each de facto prop is imbued with a preemptive subjectivity that signals an even more abrupt and radical figure-ground shift than any of the artist's exteriorized formal and conceptual inversions. Could it be that we are all just subroutines of Sean Duffy's personal matrix? Making this essay what? That cat that Neo sees in the hallway? Its déjà vu all over again!

This is where Duffy's work suspends us: between worlds, between cycles, between piston strokes, between repetitions of a locked groove. A fragment of a song overheard while lying facedown on shag carpeting in a suburban basement at the age of 11 can be as qualitatively and quantifiably meaningful as Beethoven's 9th or the cathedral at Chartres, all depending on where you stand. However persuaded we might be by the formal or conceptual elegance of an artifact, or by the weight of authority or consensus that stands behind it, it is its ability to swing both ways that causes us to recognize it as art. Sean Duffy's trying to get a message to himself. You are the missing link.

Since graduating with an MFA in painting from UCLA in 1994, DOUG HARVEY has written extensively about the Los Angeles and International art scenes and other aspects of popular culture, primarily as the art critic for *LA WEEKLY*, the largest circulation free weekly newspaper in America, and *Art Issues*, the highly respected LA-based journal of art and contemporary culture, which ceased publication in 2002. His writing has also appeared in *Art in America*, *The New York Times*, *The Nation*, *Modern Painter*, *ArtReview*, and numerous other publications. He has written museum and gallery catalog essays for Jim Shaw, Jeffrey Vallance, Camille Rose Garcia, Tim Hawkinson, Marnie Weber, Don Suggs, Lari Pittman, Georganne Deen, Rick Griffin, Gary Panter, Margaret Keane, Ed "Big Daddy" Roth, Thomas Kinkade, Basil Wolverton and many others.

Harvey lives and works in Los Angeles and maintains a blog at WWW.DOUGHARVEY.BLOGSPOT.COM and a website at WWW.DOUGHARVEY.LA.

PLATES

S&AN RECORDS

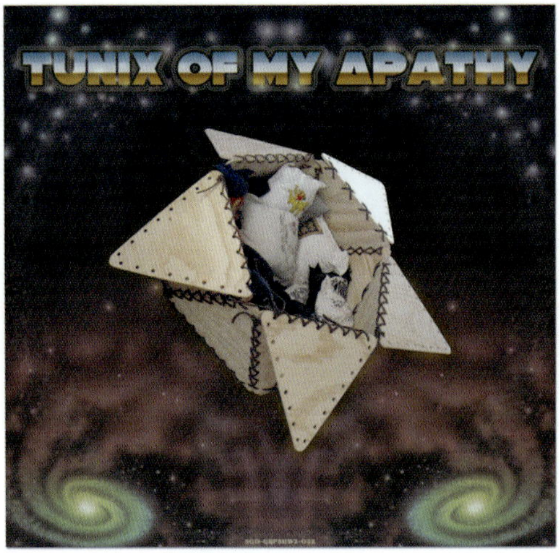
TUNIX OF MY APATHY

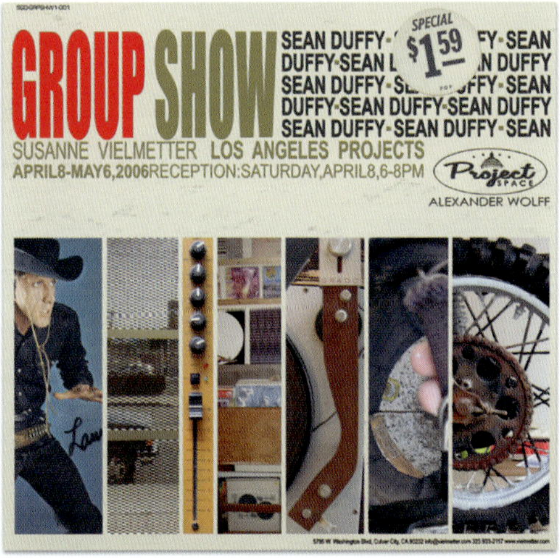
GROUP SHOW
SEAN DUFFY·
FY·SEAN
DUFFY·SEAN
N DUFFY
SEAN DUFFY·SE
FFY·SEAN
DUFFY·SEAN DUFFY·SEAN DUFFY
SEAN DUFFY·SEAN DUFFY·SEAN
SPECIAL
$1.59
SUSANNE VIELMETTER LOS ANGELES PROJECTS
APRIL8-MAY6,2006RECEPTION:SATURDAY,APRIL8,6-8PM
Project SPACE
ALEXANDER WOLFF

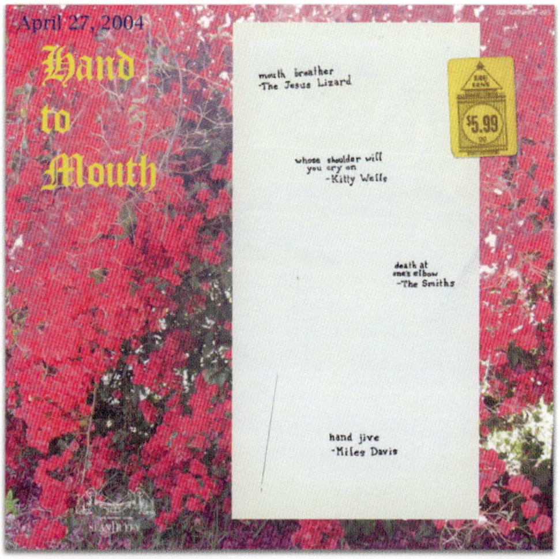
April 27, 2004
Hand to Mouth
mouth breather
-The Jesus Lizard
$5.99
whose shoulder will you cry on
-Kitty Wells
death at ones elbow
-The Smiths
hand jive
-Miles Davis

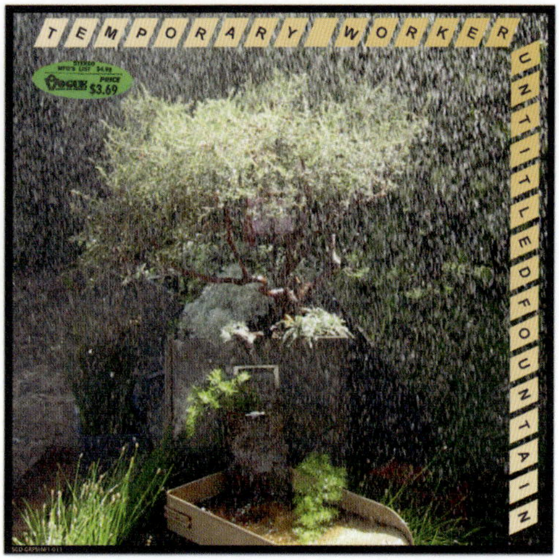
TEMPORARY WORKER
UNTITLEDFOUNTAIN
$3.69

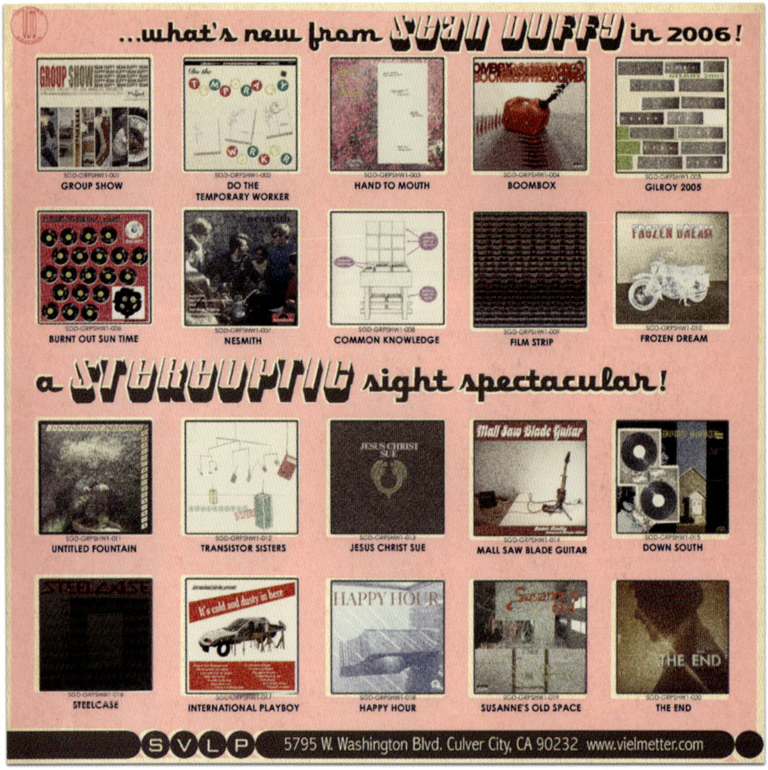

...what's new from SEAN DUFFY in 2006!
GROUP SHOW
DO THE TEMPORARY WORKER
HAND TO MOUTH
BOOMBOX
GILROY 2005
BURNT OUT SUN TIME
NESMITH
COMMON KNOWLEDGE
FILM STRIP
FROZEN DREAM
a STEREOPTIC sight spectacular!
UNTITLED FOUNTAIN
TRANSISTOR SISTERS
JESUS CHRIST SUE
MALL SAW BLADE GUITAR
DOWN SOUTH
STEELCASE
INTERNATIONAL PLAYBOY
HAPPY HOUR
SUSANNE'S OLD SPACE
THE END
SVLP
5795 W. Washington Blvd. Culver City, CA 90232 www.vielmetter.com

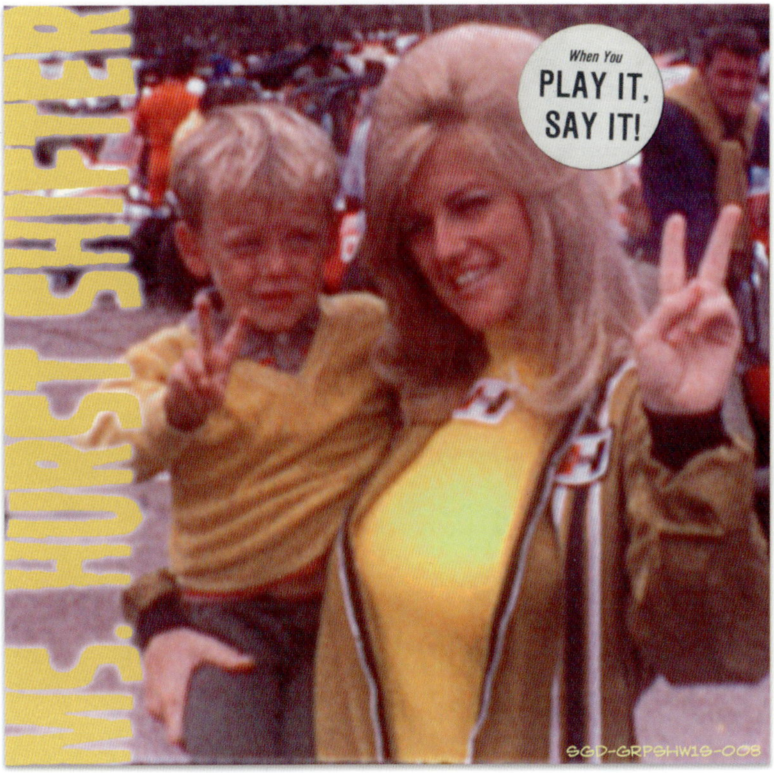
MS. HURST SHIFTER
When You
PLAY IT,
SAY IT!
SGD-GRPSHW1S-008

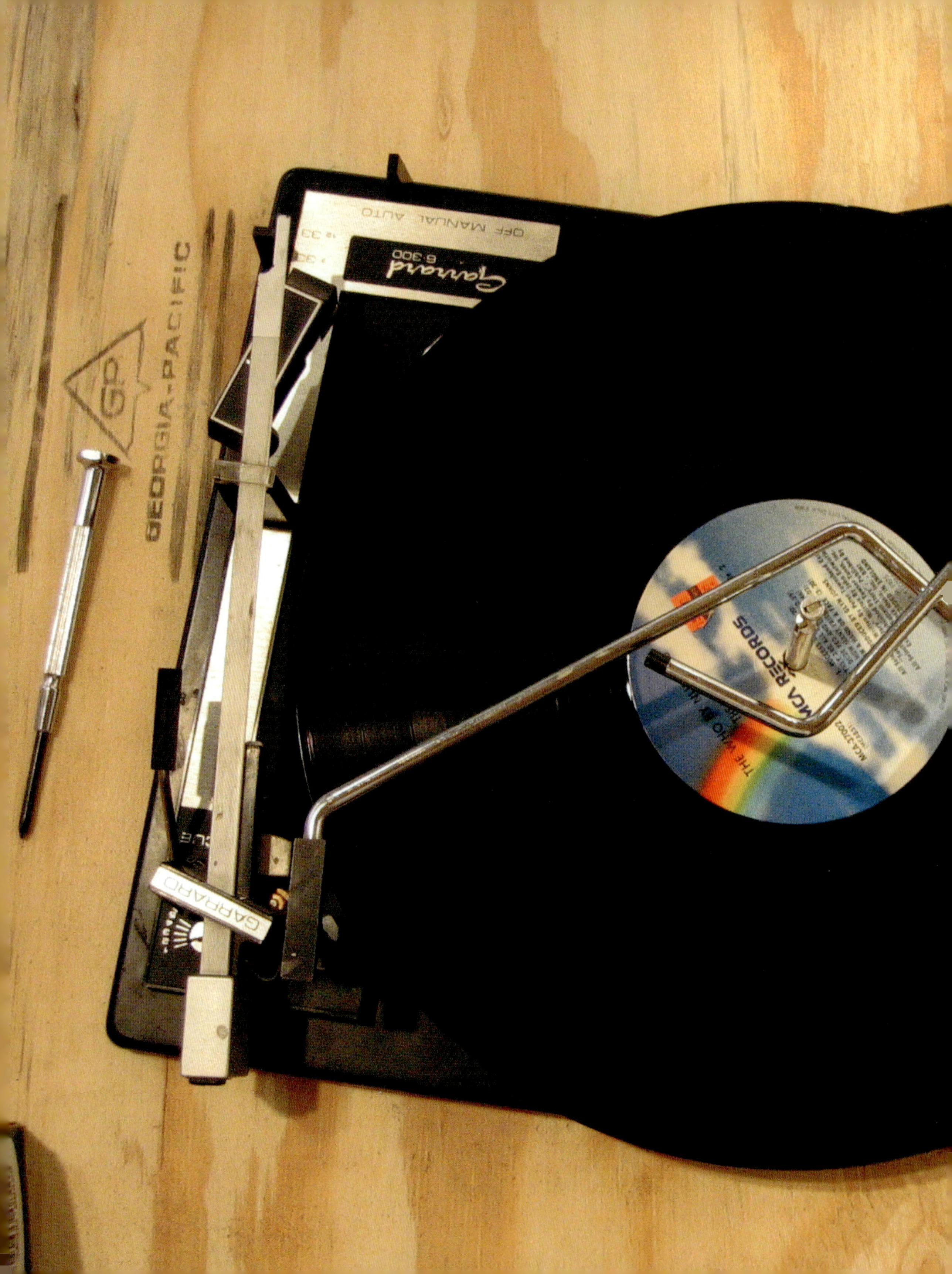

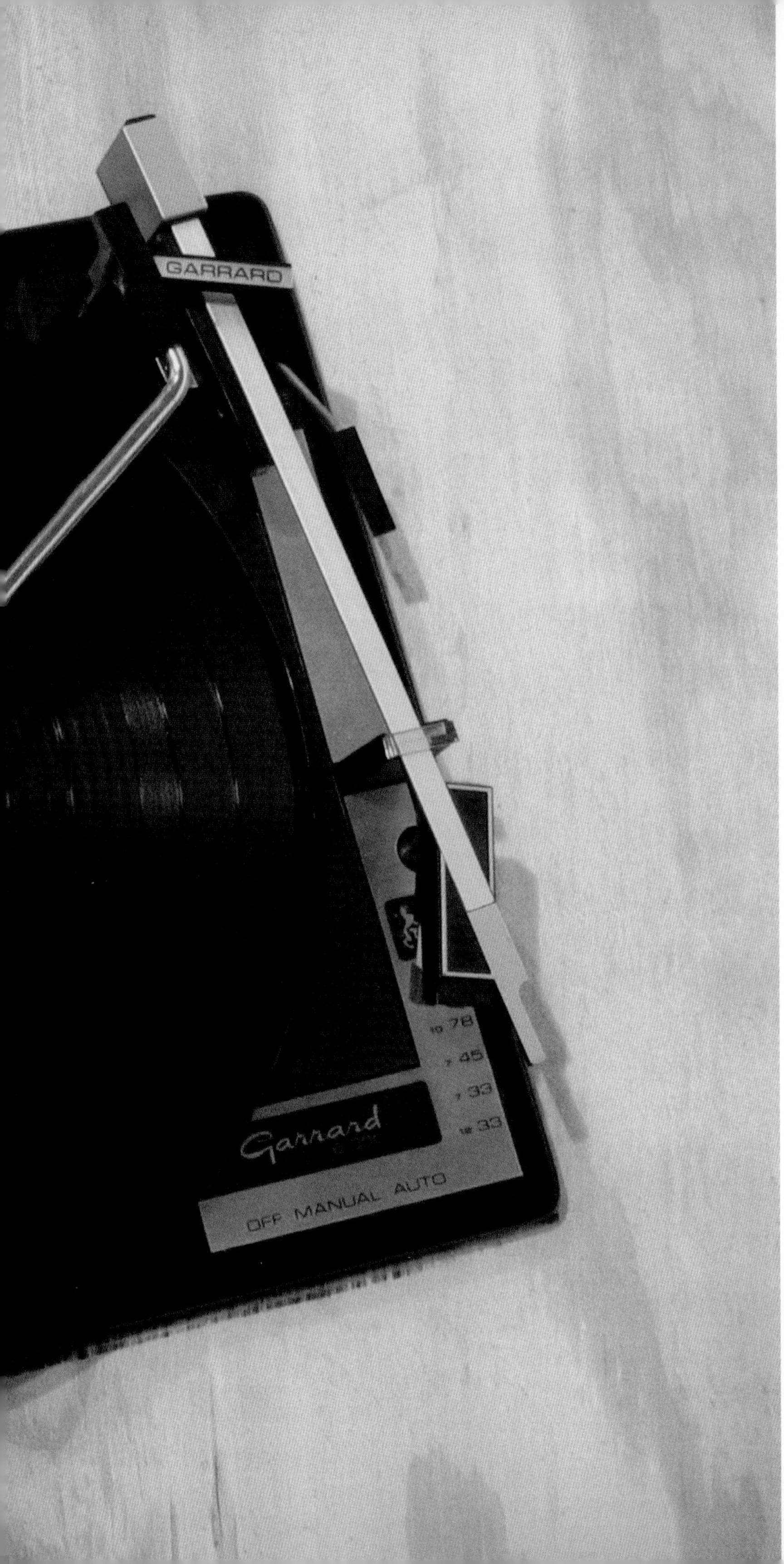
GARRARD
78
45
33
33
Garrard
OFF MANUAL AUTO

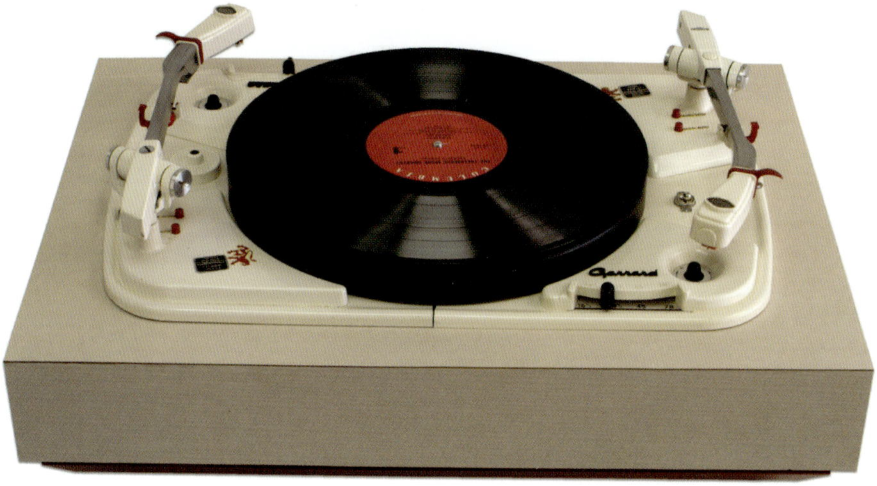

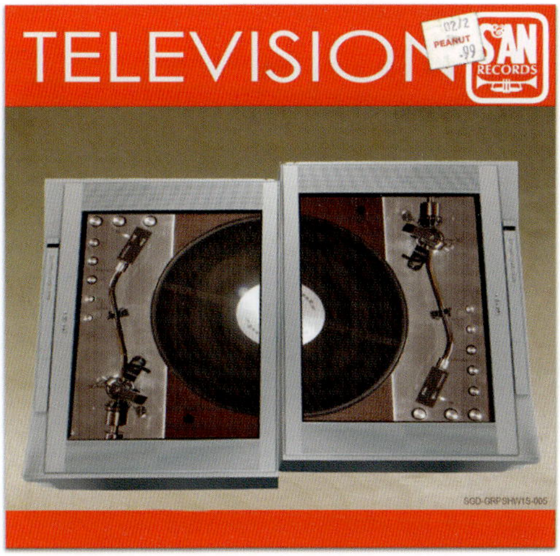
TELEVISION
02/2
PEANUT
.99
RECORDS
SGD-GRPSHW15-005

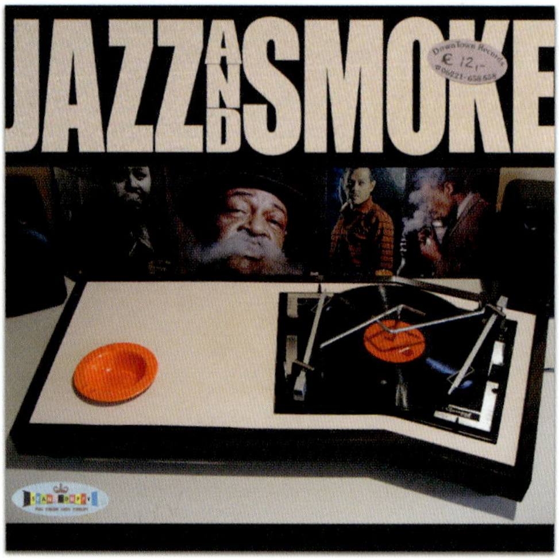
JAZZ AND SMOKE

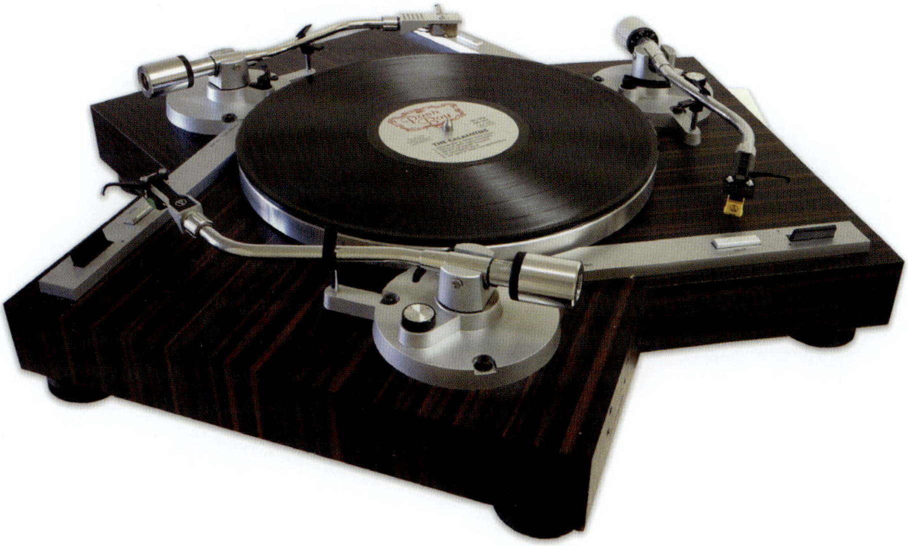

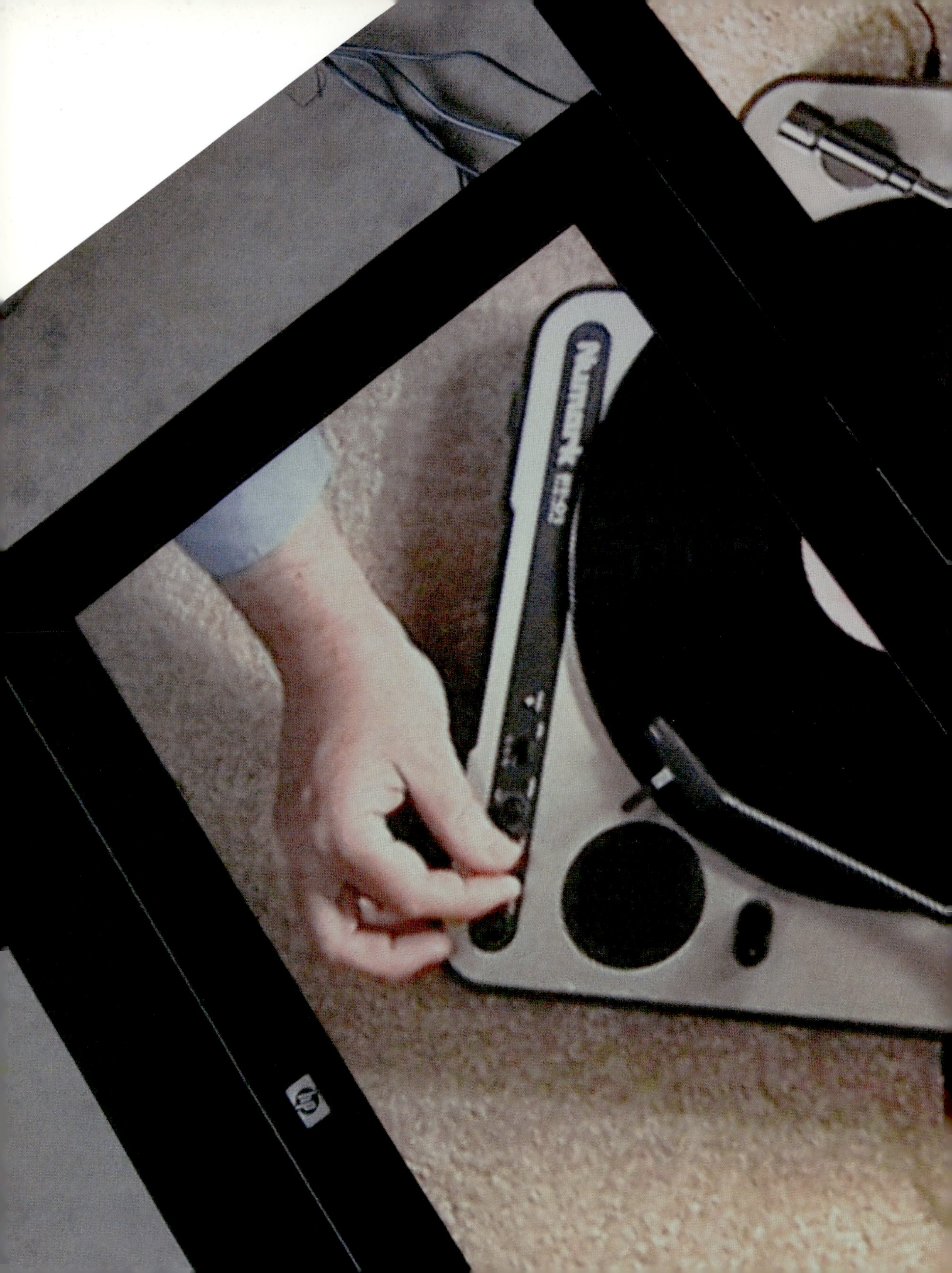
Numark

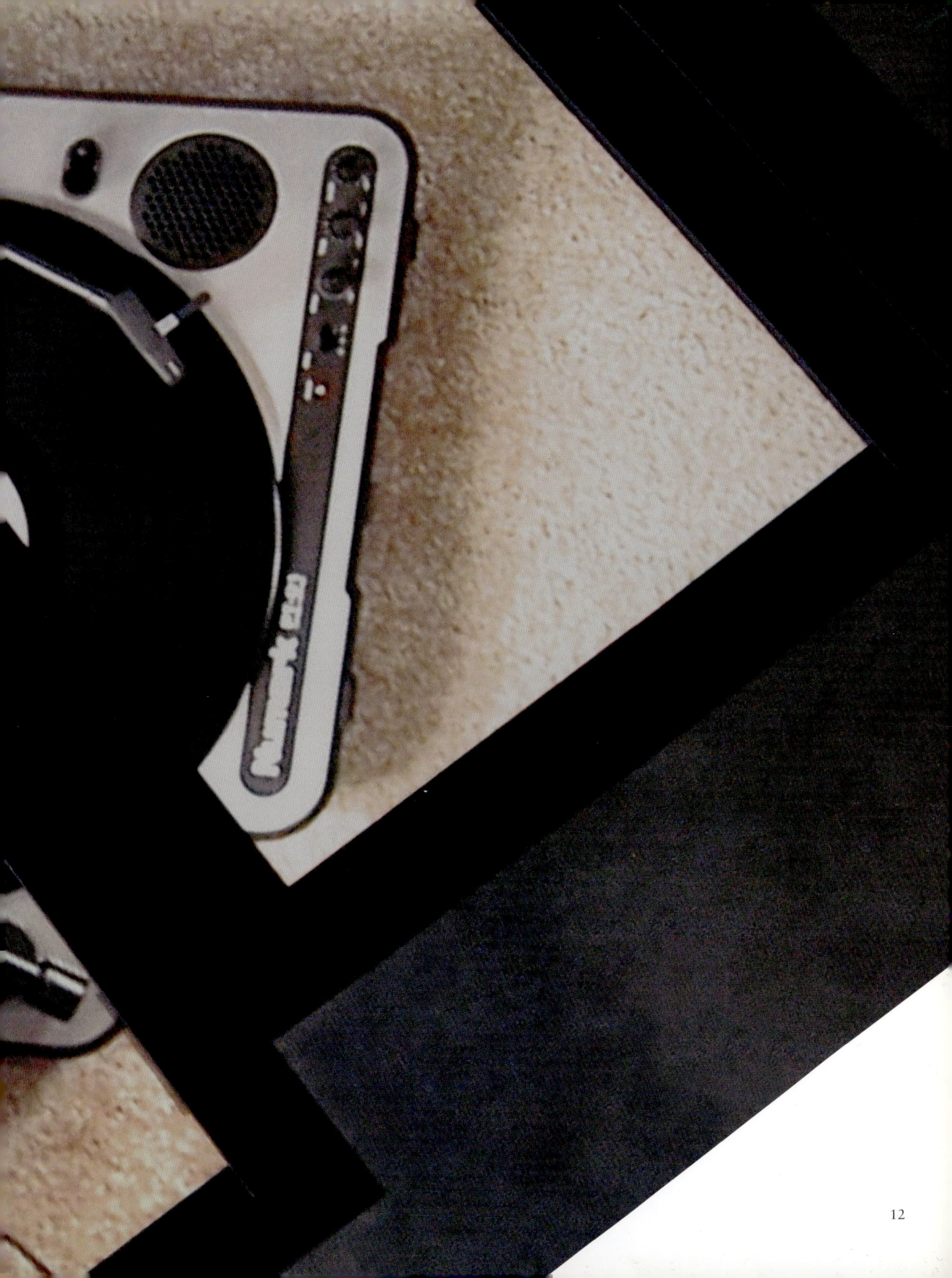

SEAND

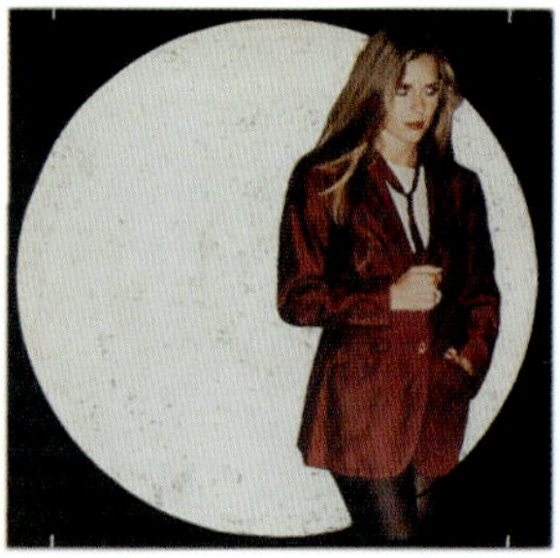
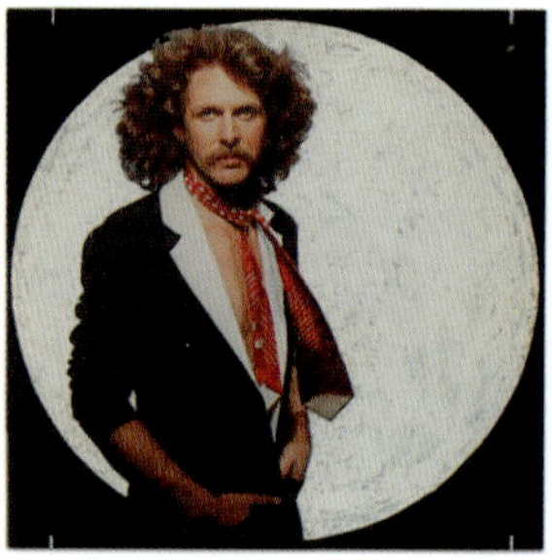
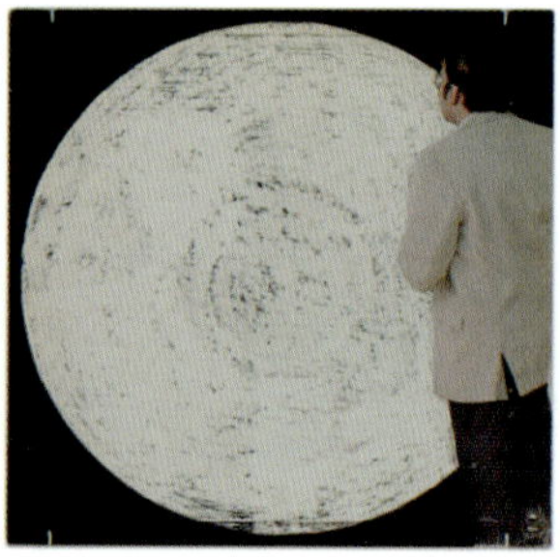

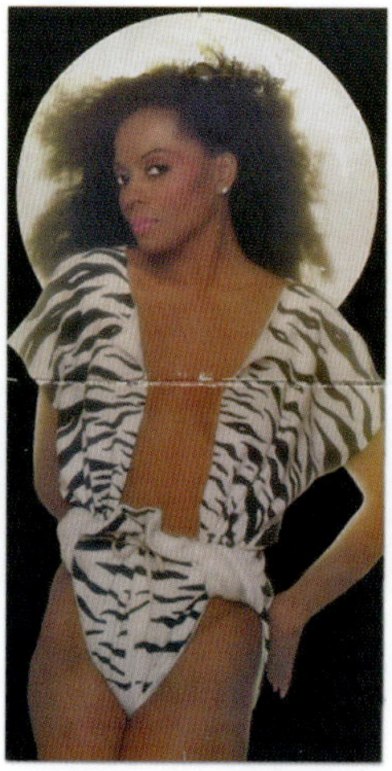
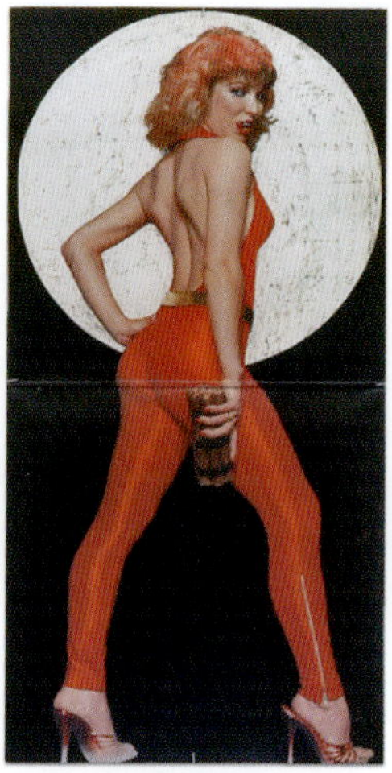
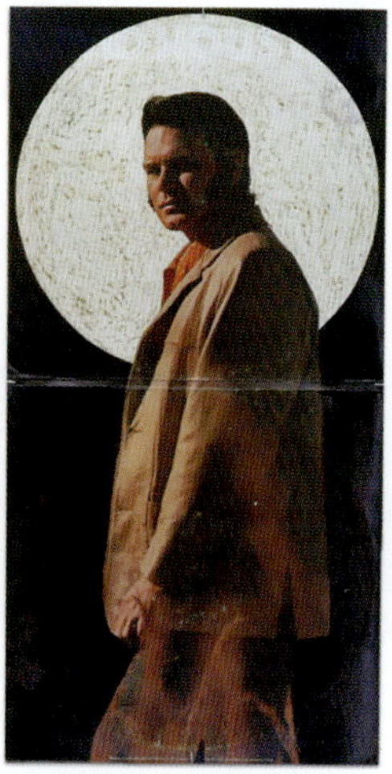

14 | 15 | 16

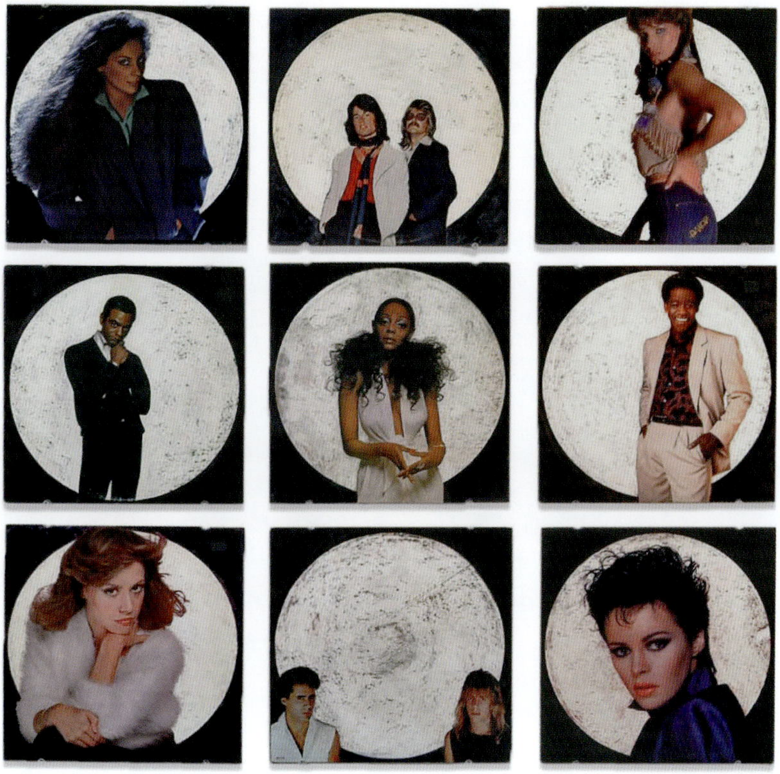

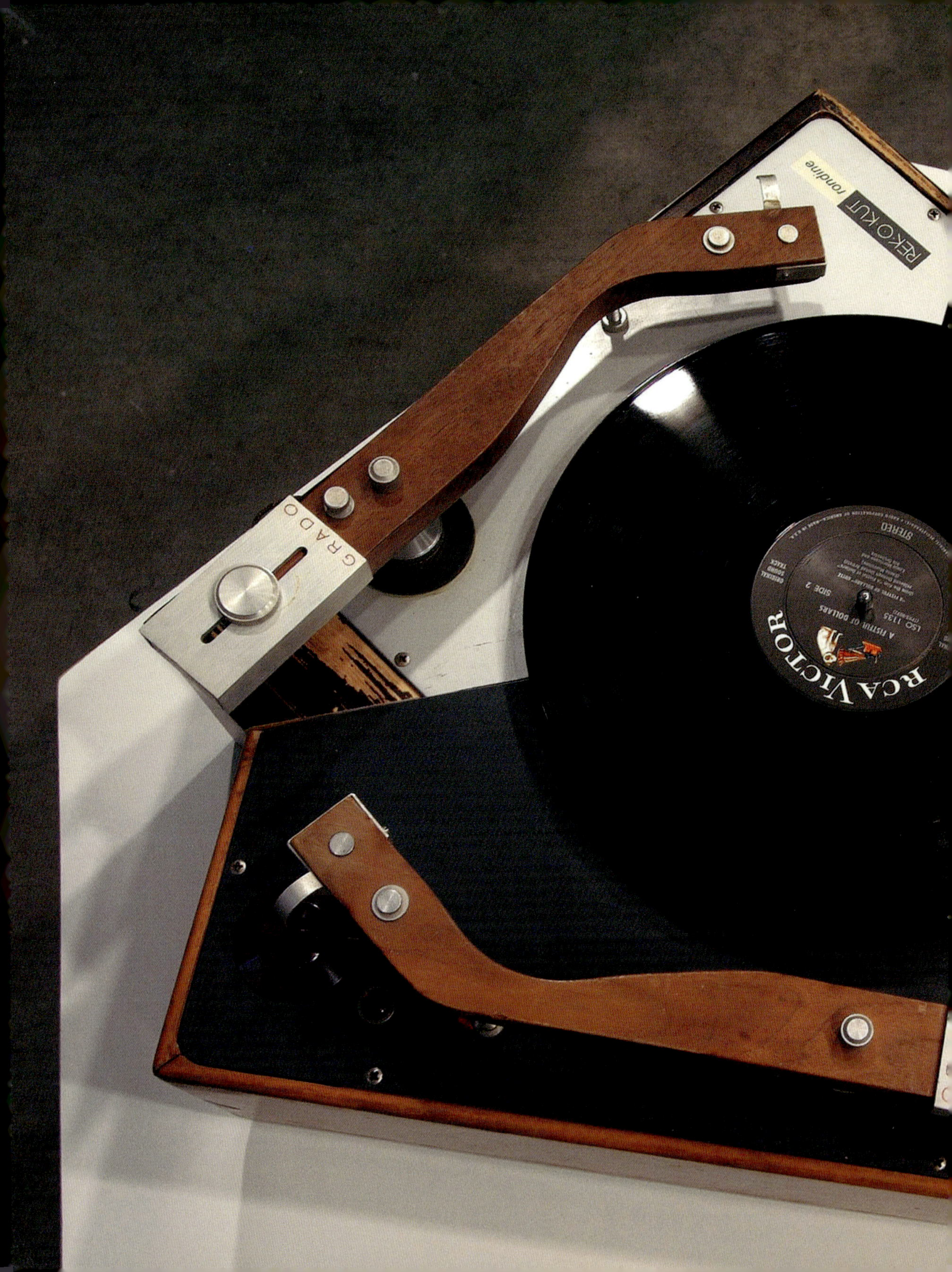
REK-O-KUT
rondine
GRADO
RCA Victor

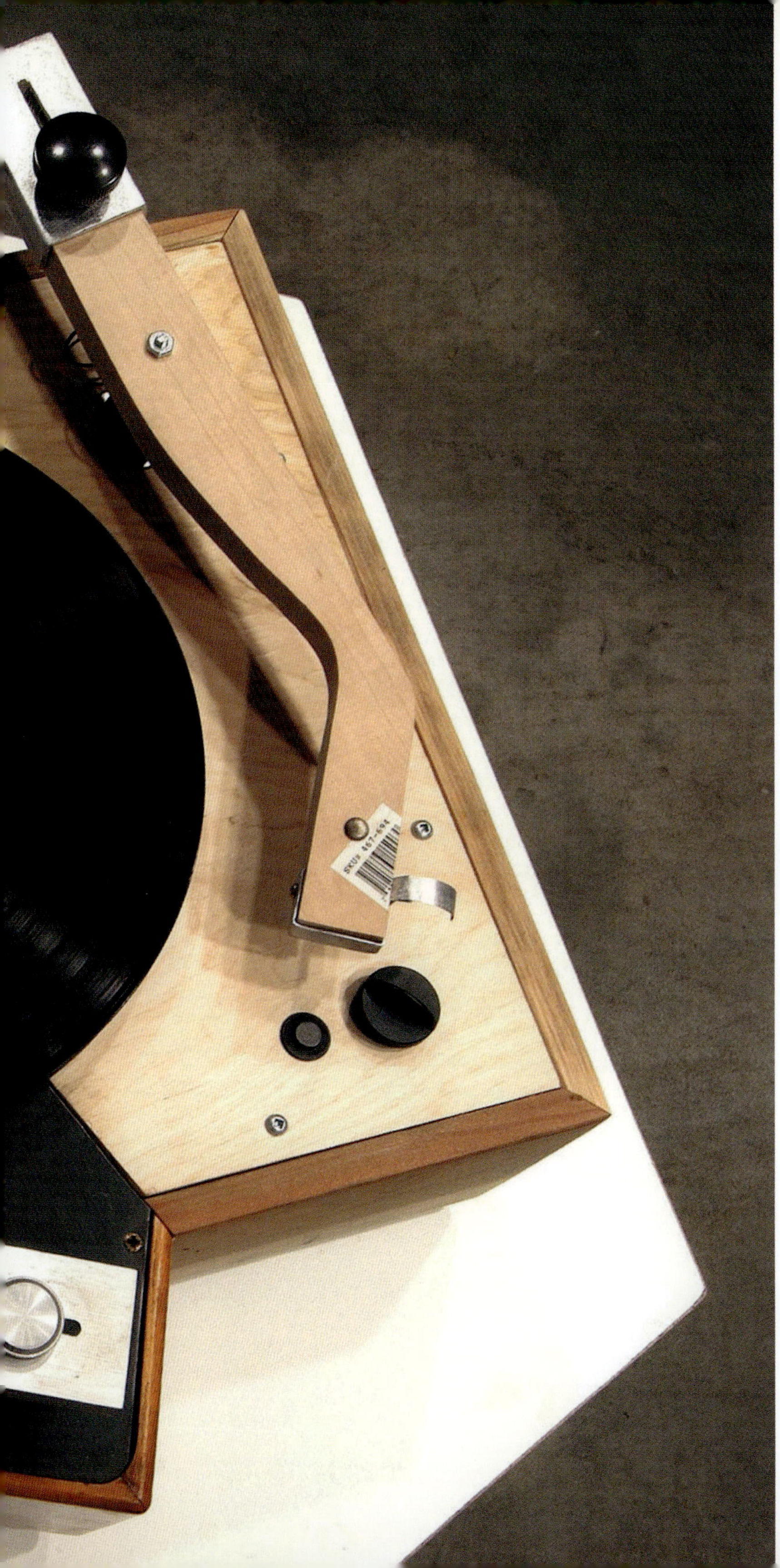

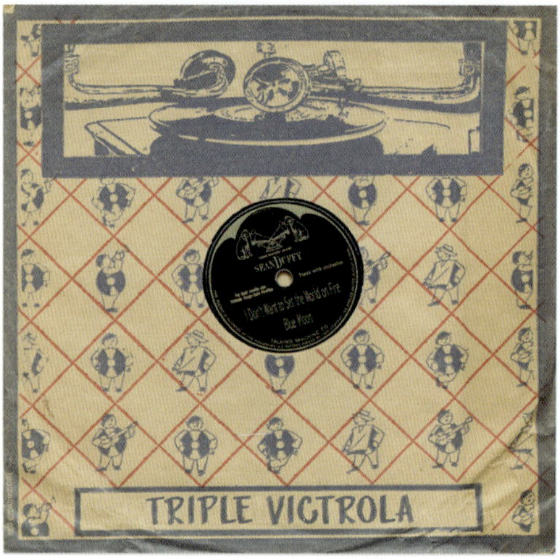
SEAN DUFFY
I Don't Want to Set the World on Fire
Blue Moon
TRIPLE VICTROLA

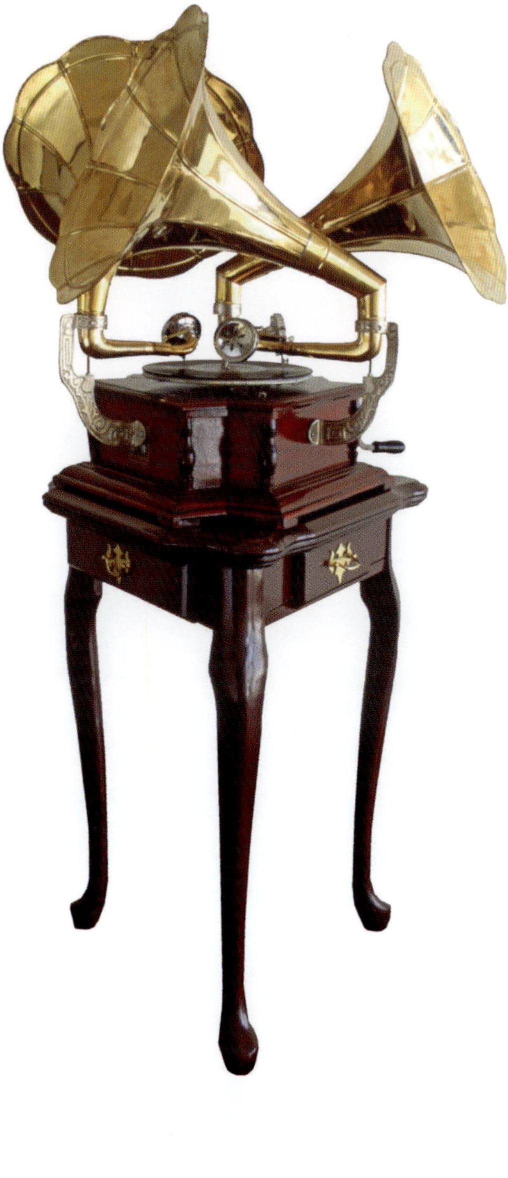

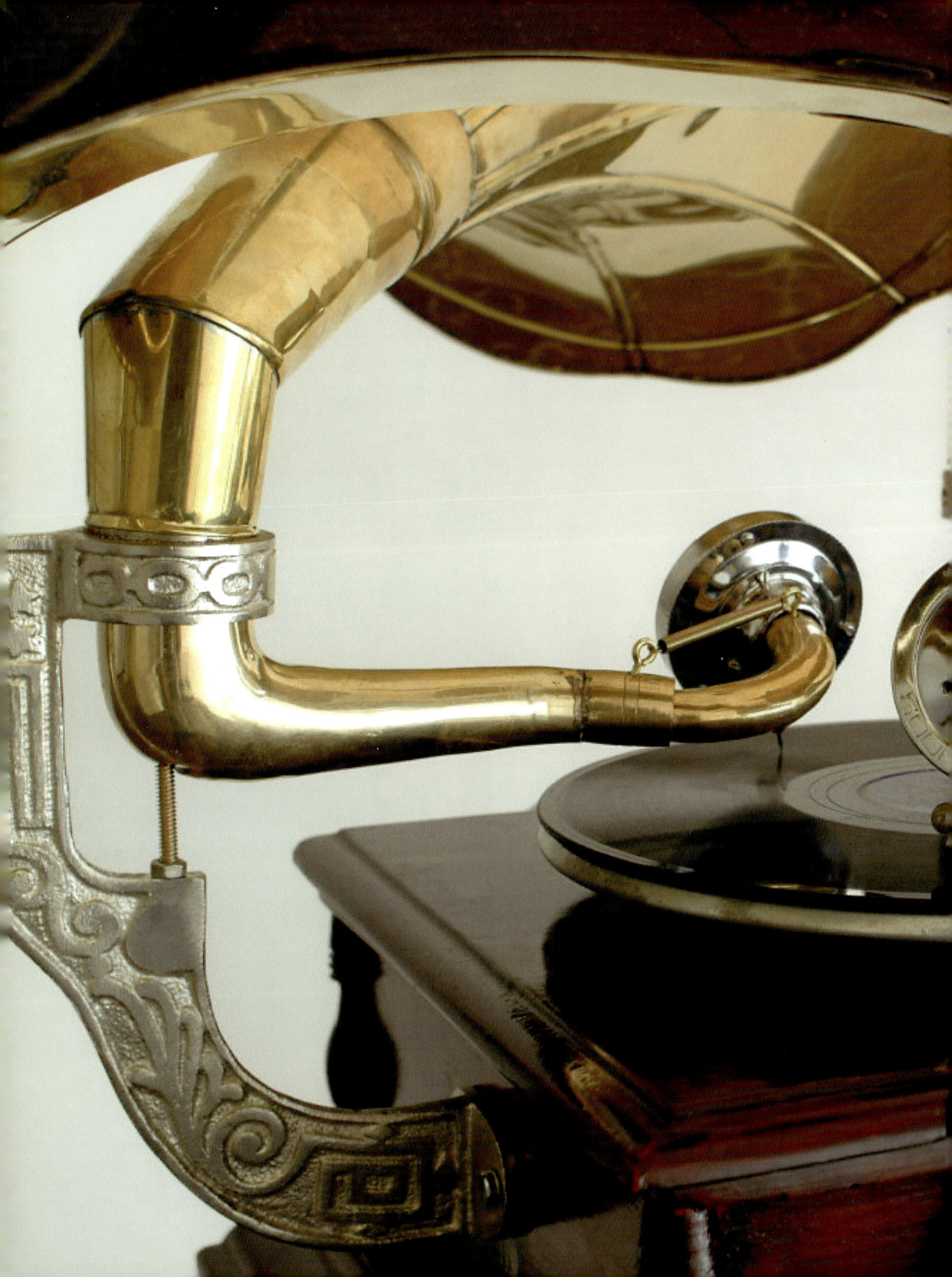

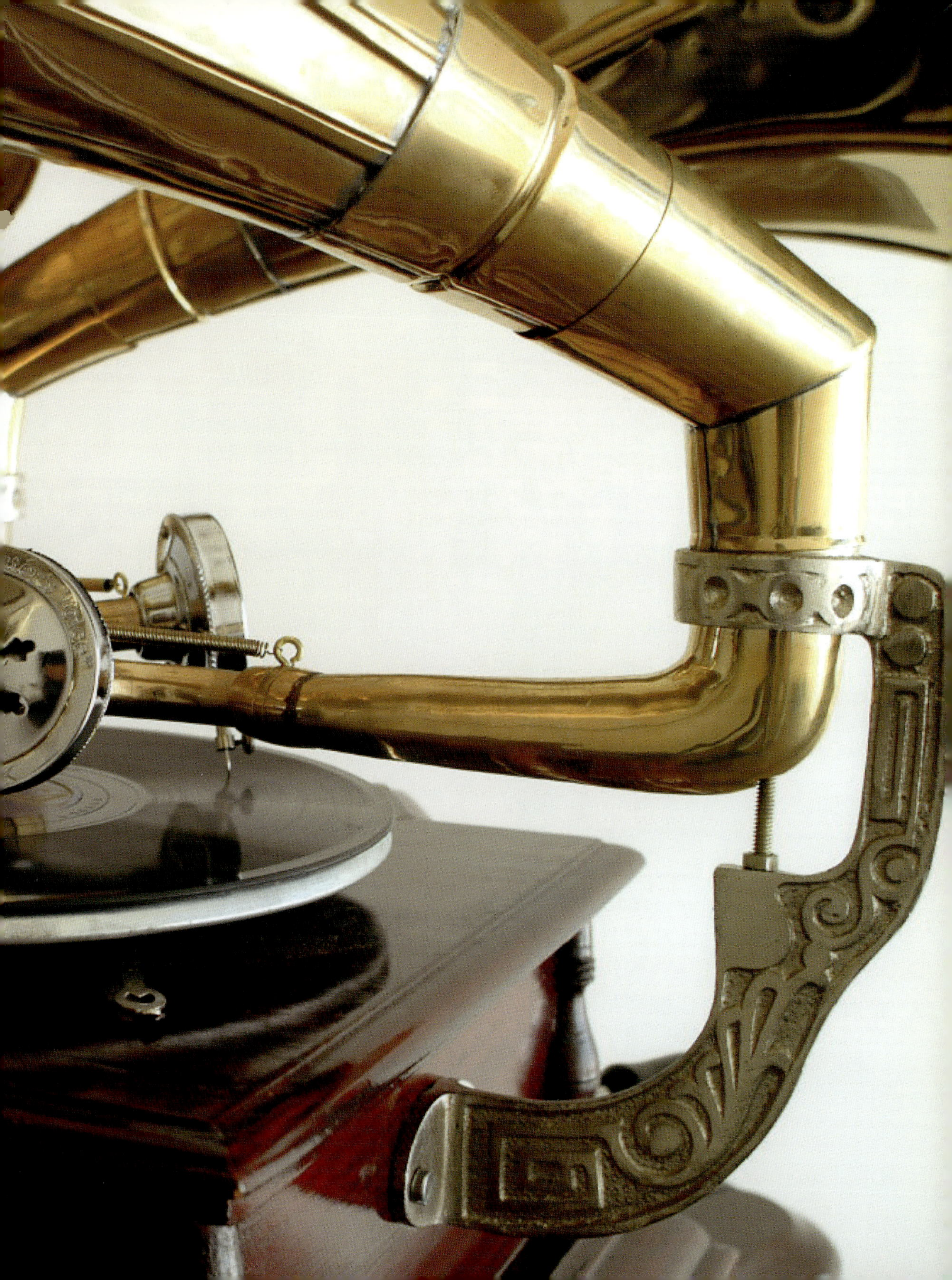

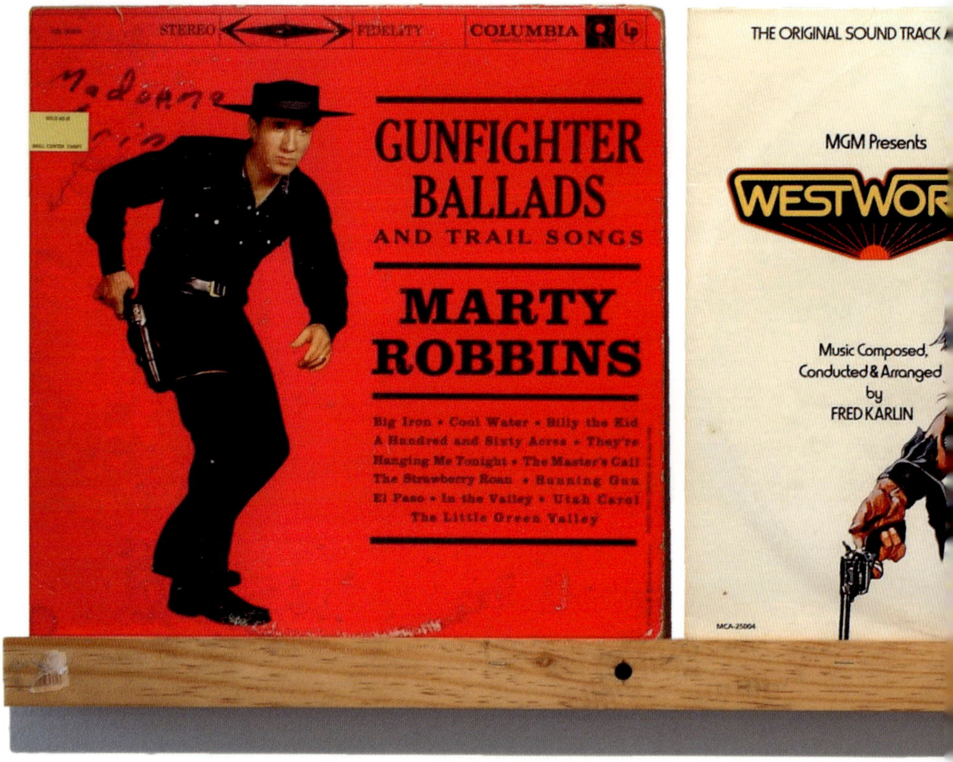
STEREO FIDELITY
COLUMBIA
GUNFIGHTER BALLADS
AND TRAIL SONGS
MARTY ROBBINS
Big Iron • Cool Water • Billy the Kid
A Hundred and Sixty Acres • They're
Hanging Me Tonight • The Master's Call
The Strawberry Roan • Running Gun
El Paso • In the Valley • Utah Carol
The Little Green Valley
THE ORIGINAL SOUND TRACK
MGM Presents
Music Composed,
Conducted & Arranged
by
FRED KARLIN
MCA-25004

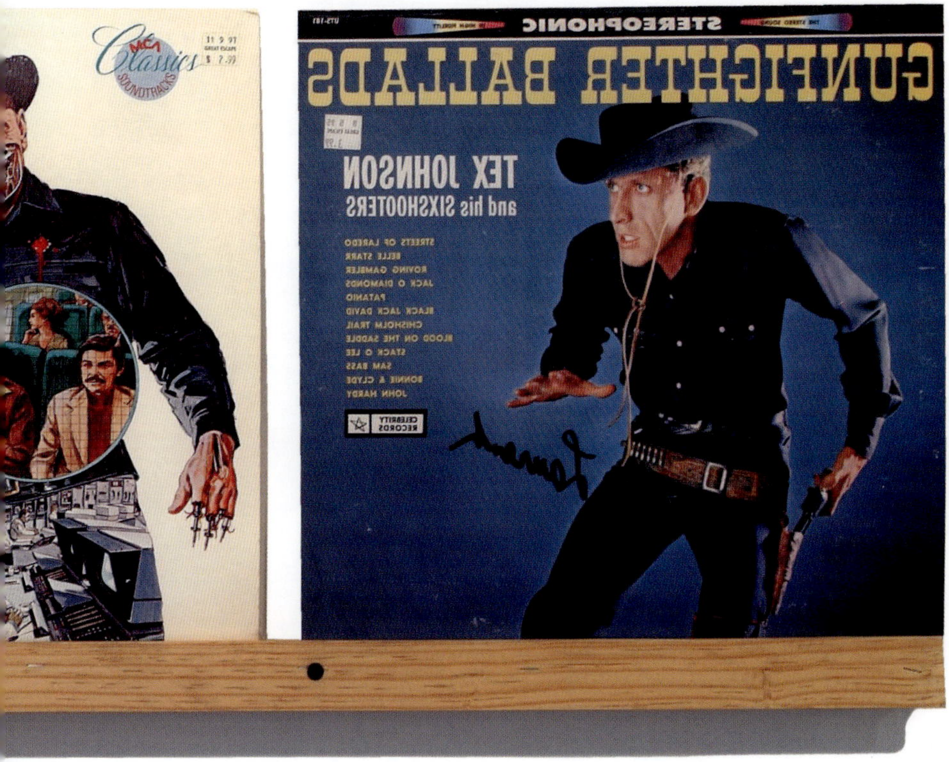
MCA Classics
SOUNDTRACKS
STEREOPHONIC
GUNFIGHTER BALLADS
TEX JOHNSON
and his SIXSHOOTERS
STREETS OF LAREDO
BELLE STARR
ROVING GAMBLER
JACK O DIAMONDS
PATANIO
BLACK JACK DAVID
CHISHOLM TRAIL
BLOOD ON THE SADDLE
STACK O LEE
SAM BASS
BONNIE & CLYDE
JOHN HARDY
CELEBRITY RECORDS

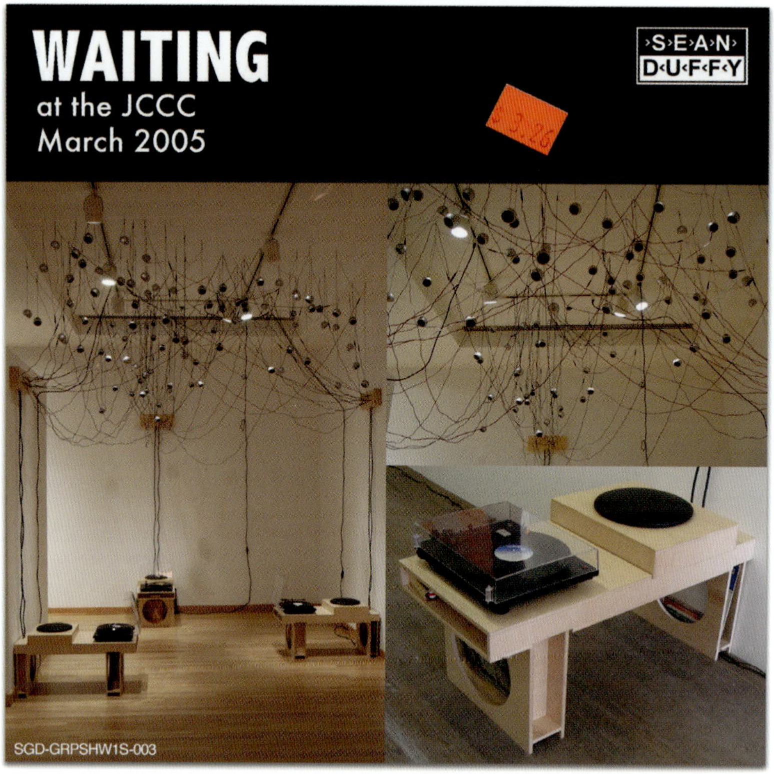
WAITING
at the JCCC
March 2005
SEAN
DUFFY
SGD-GRPSHW1S-003

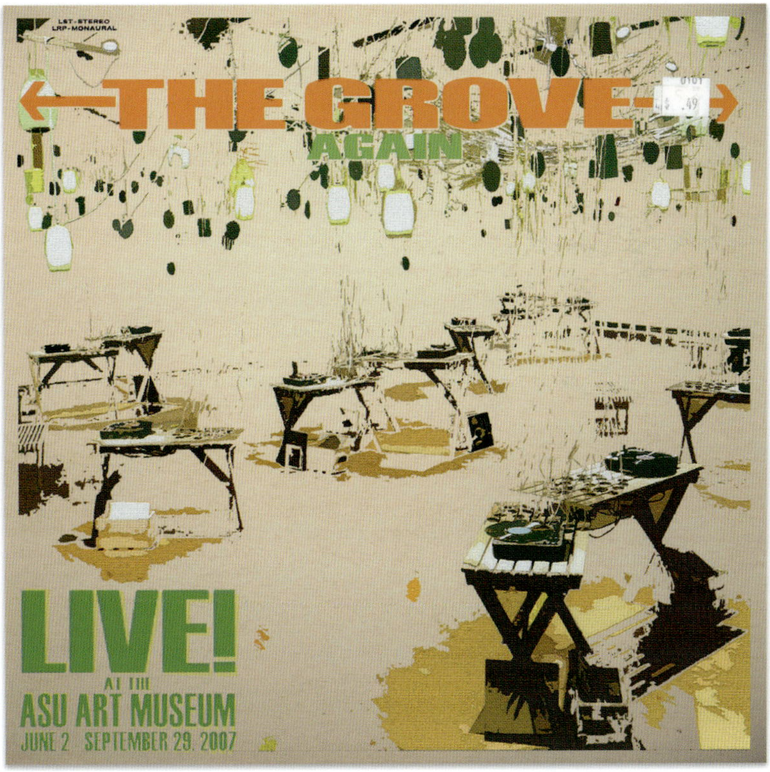
LST-STEREO
LRP-MONAURAL
THE GROVE
$ .49
AGAIN
LIVE!
AT THE
ASU ART MUSEUM
JUNE 2 SEPTEMBER 29, 2007

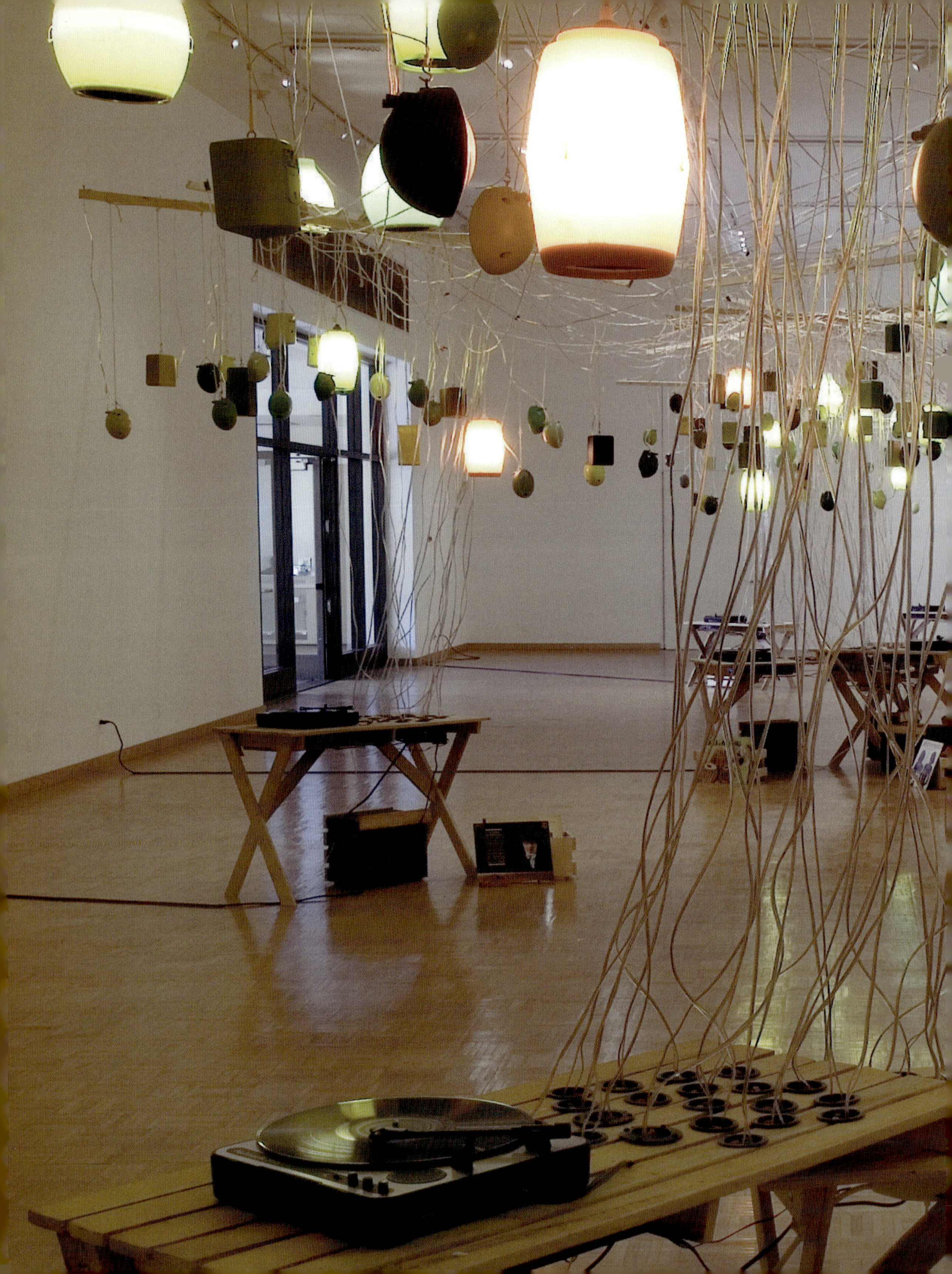

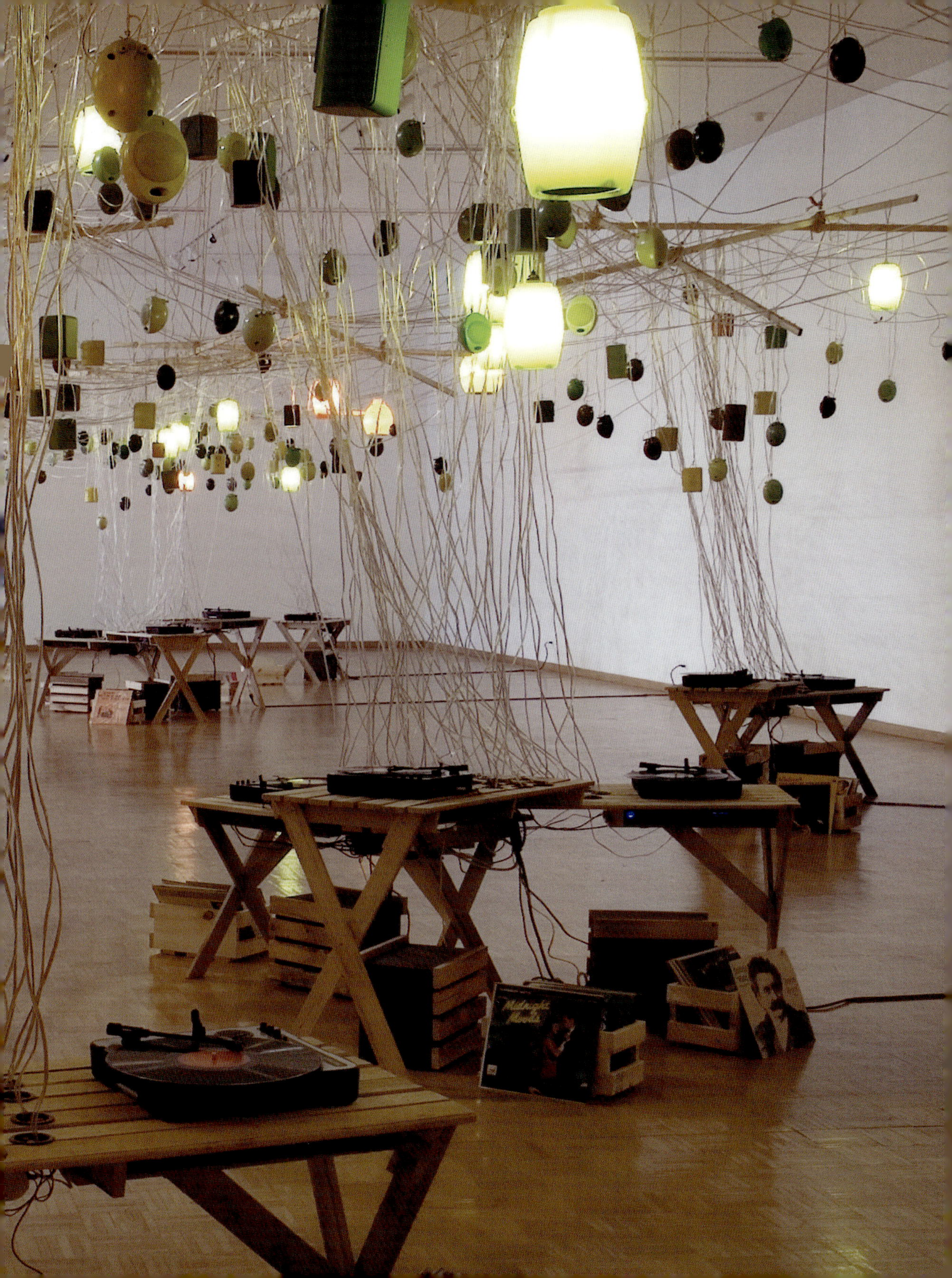

SEAN
DUFFY

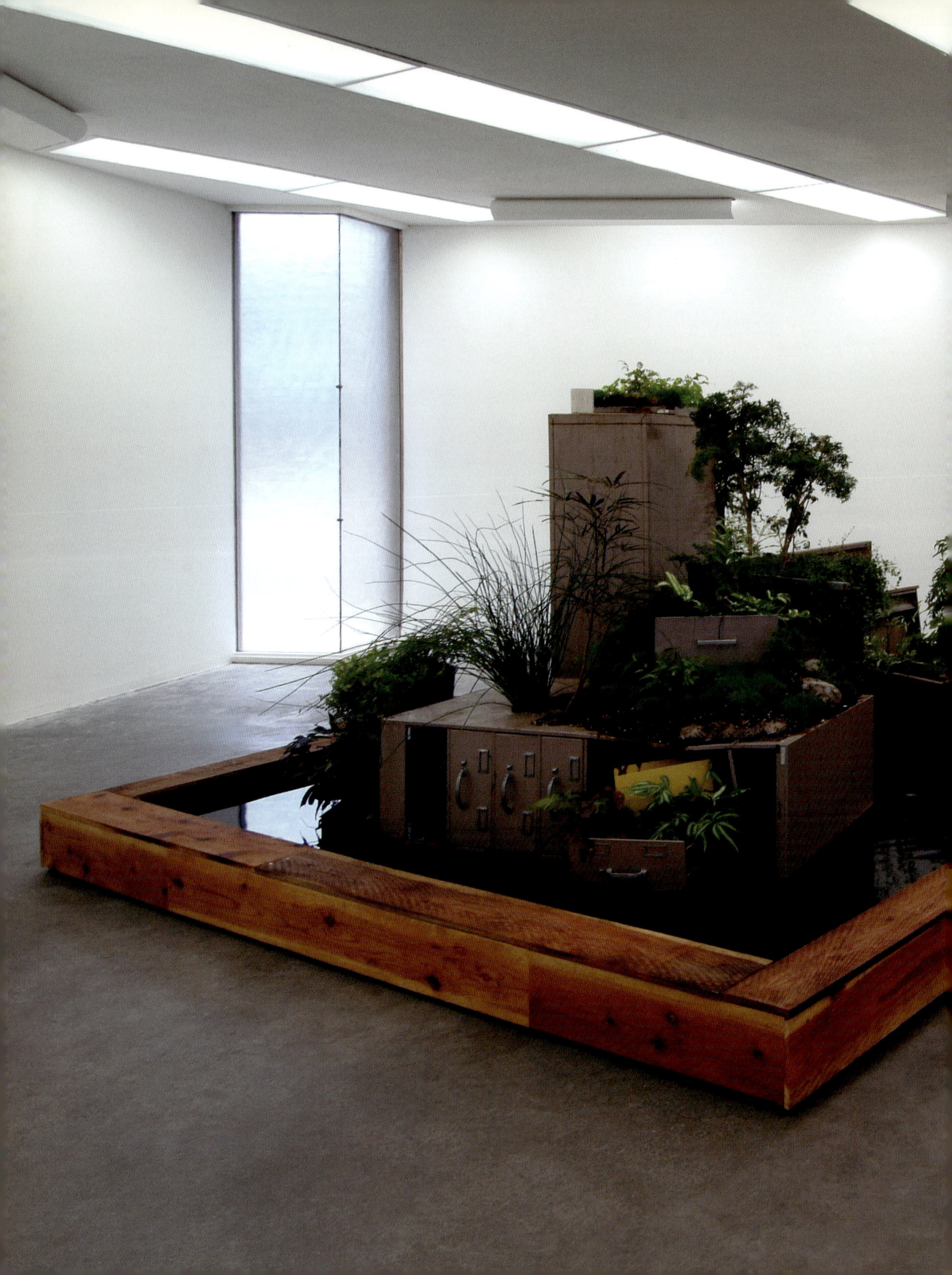

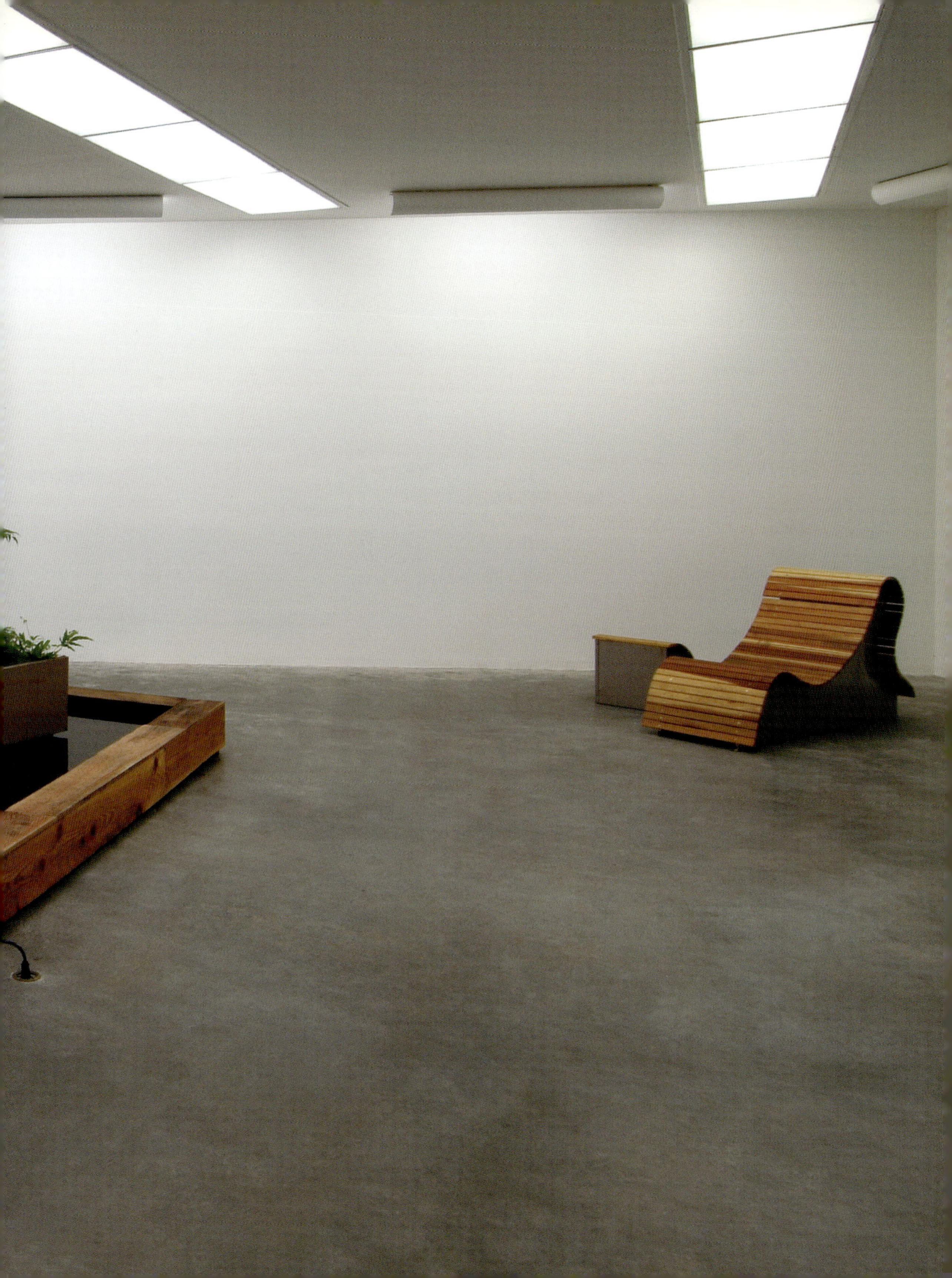

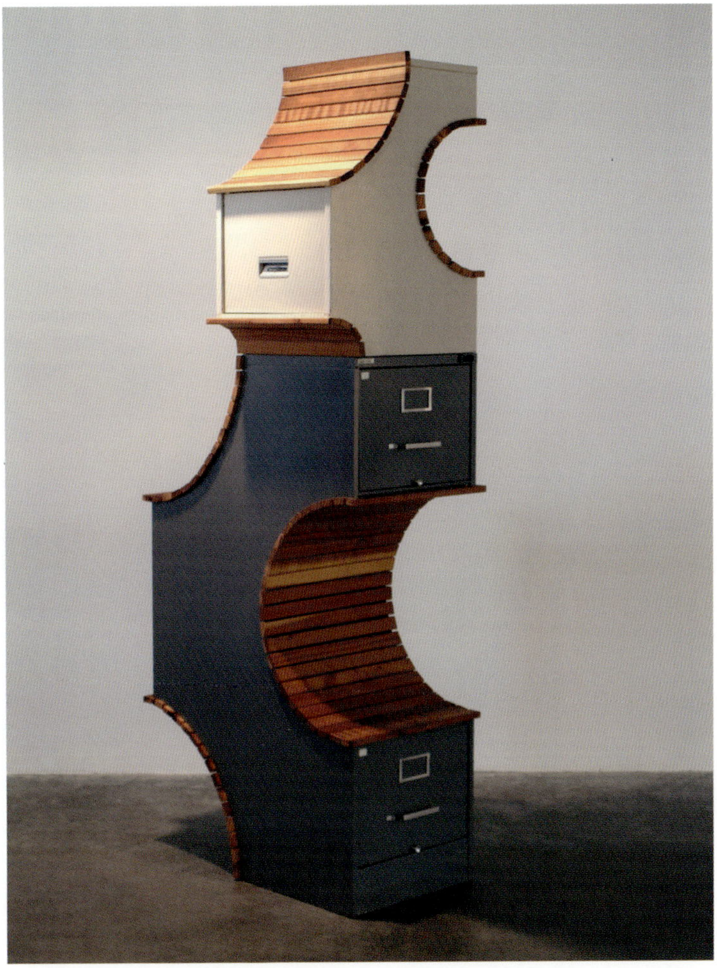

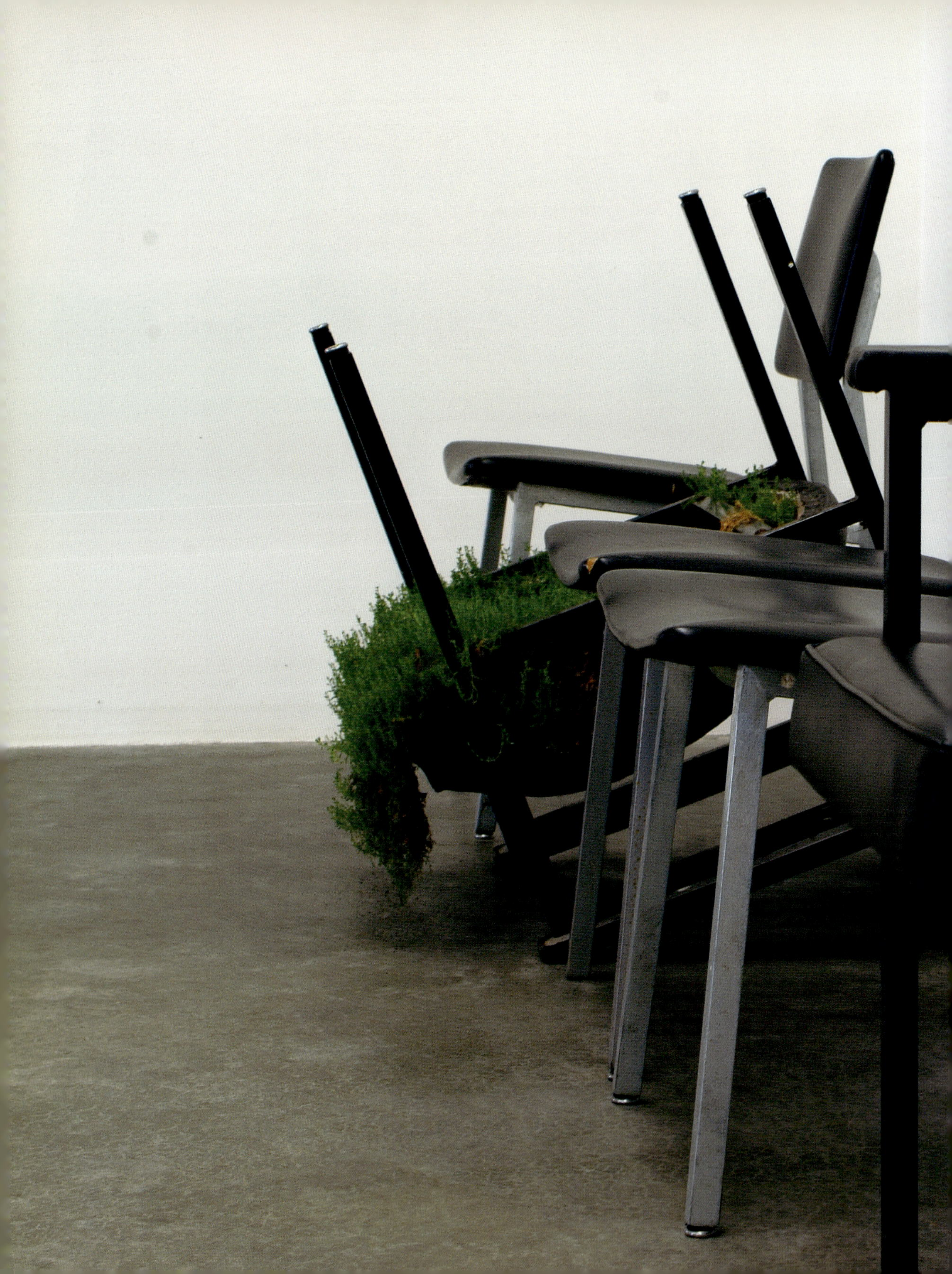

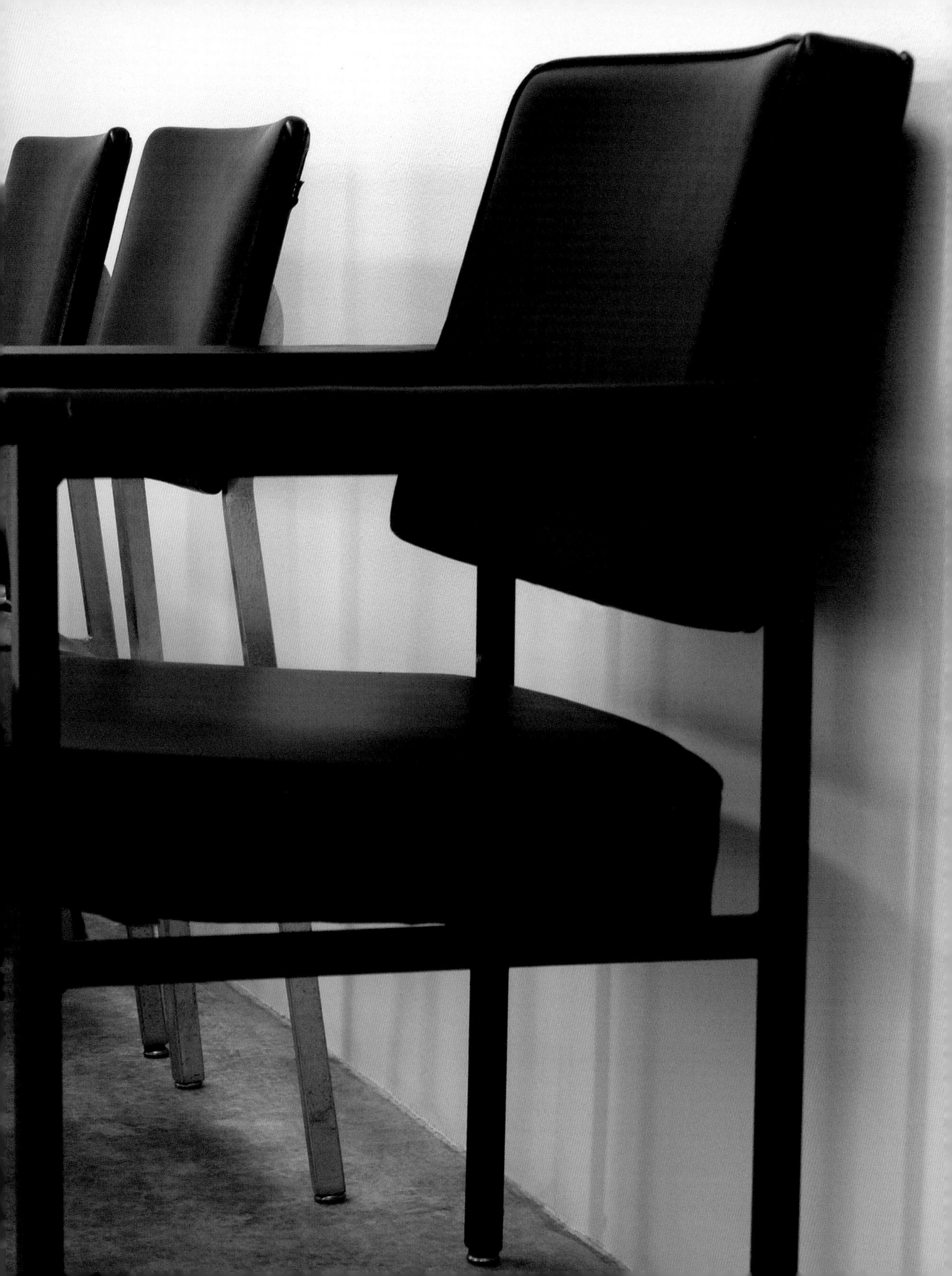

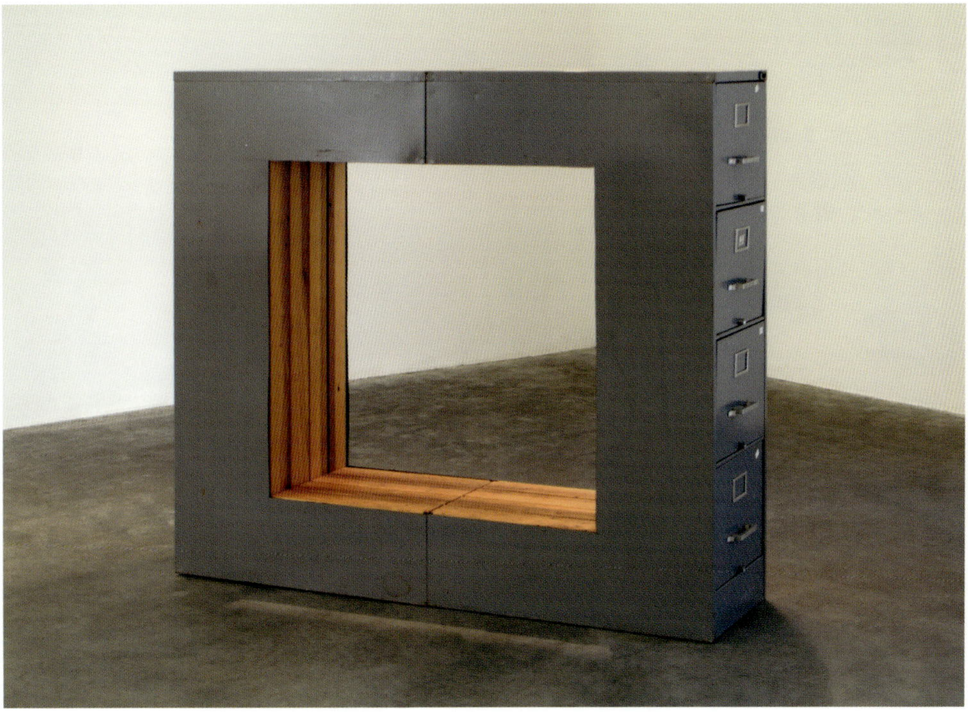

SEAN DUFFY

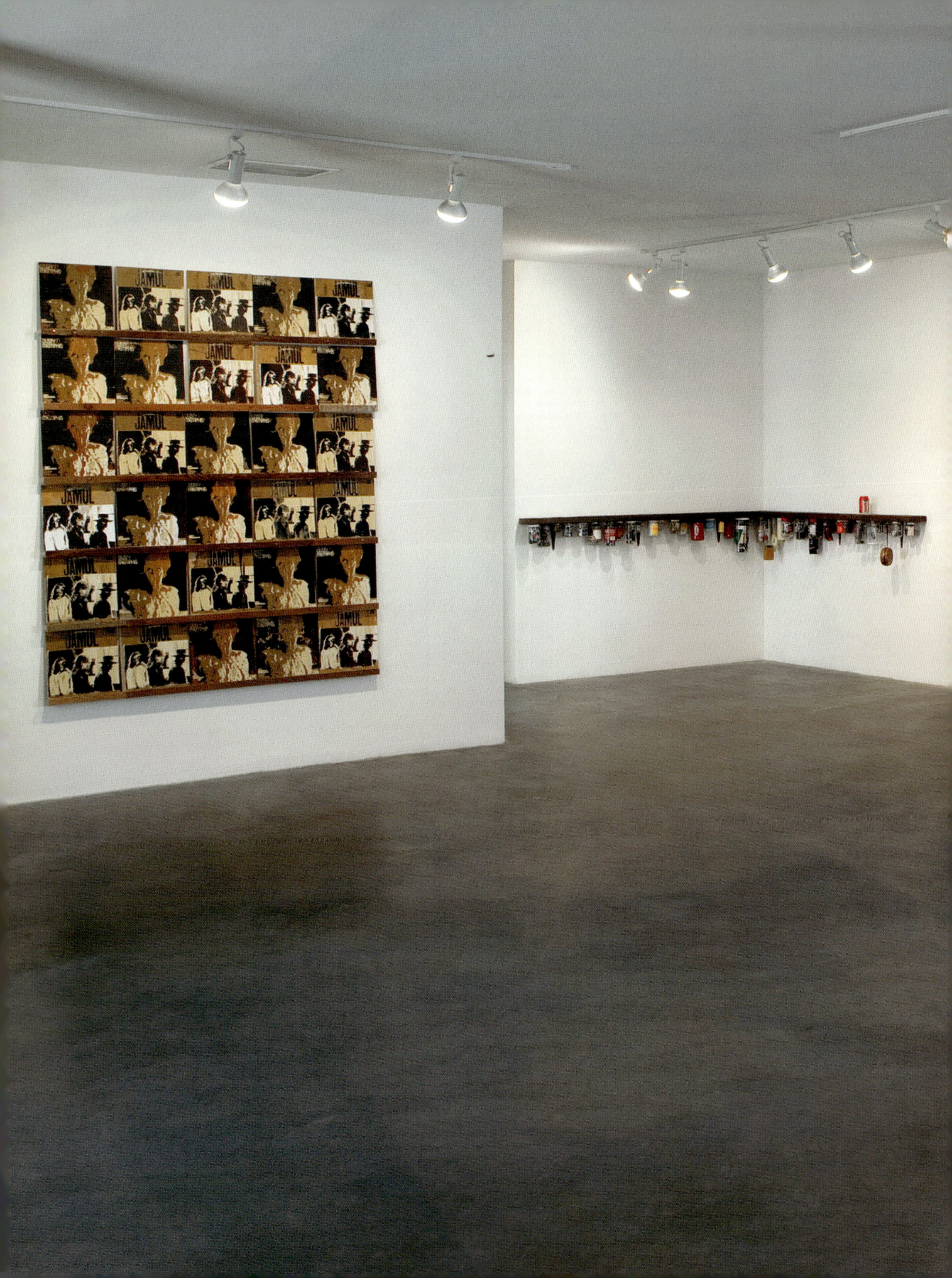
JAMUL

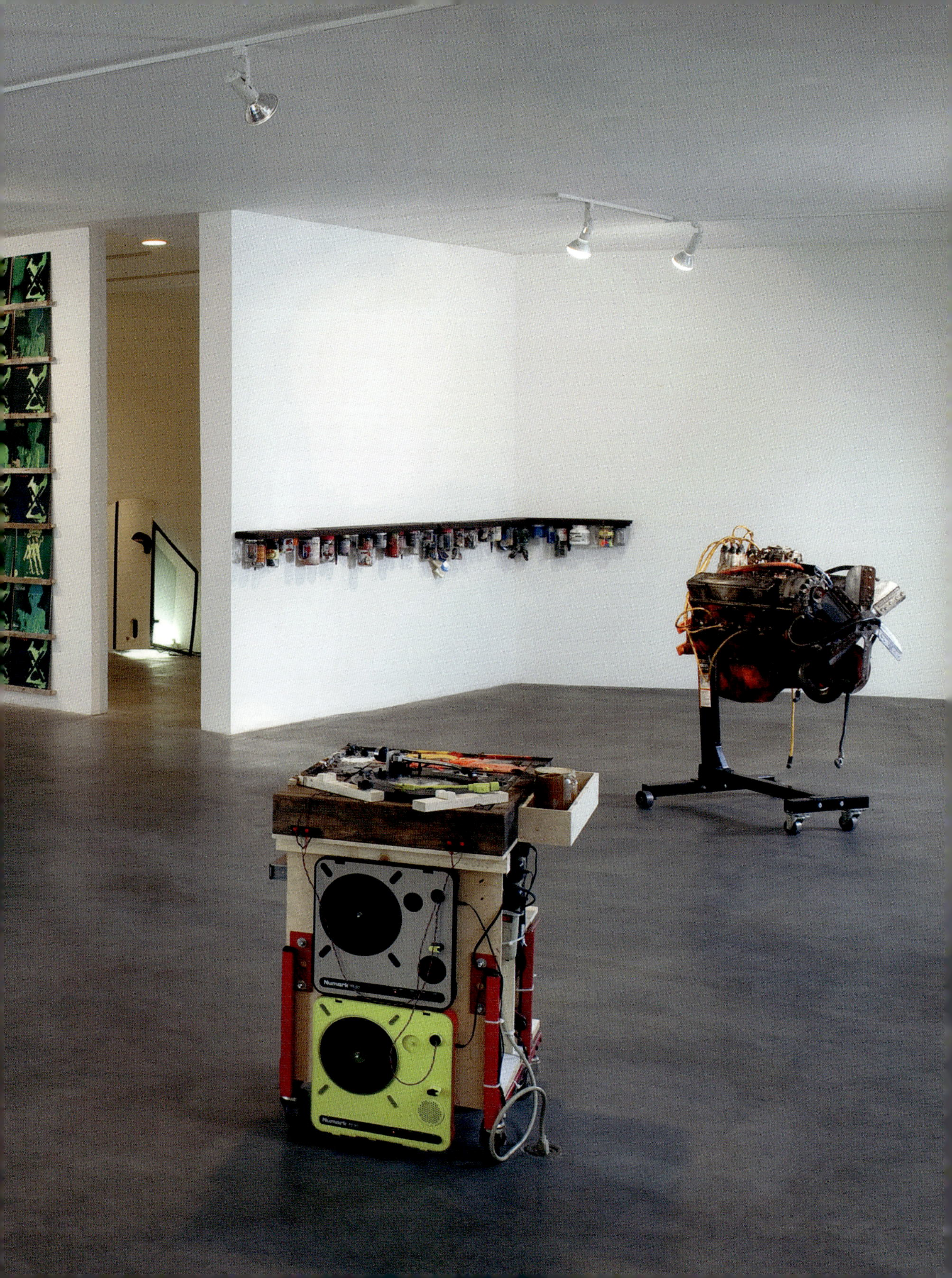
Numark
Numark

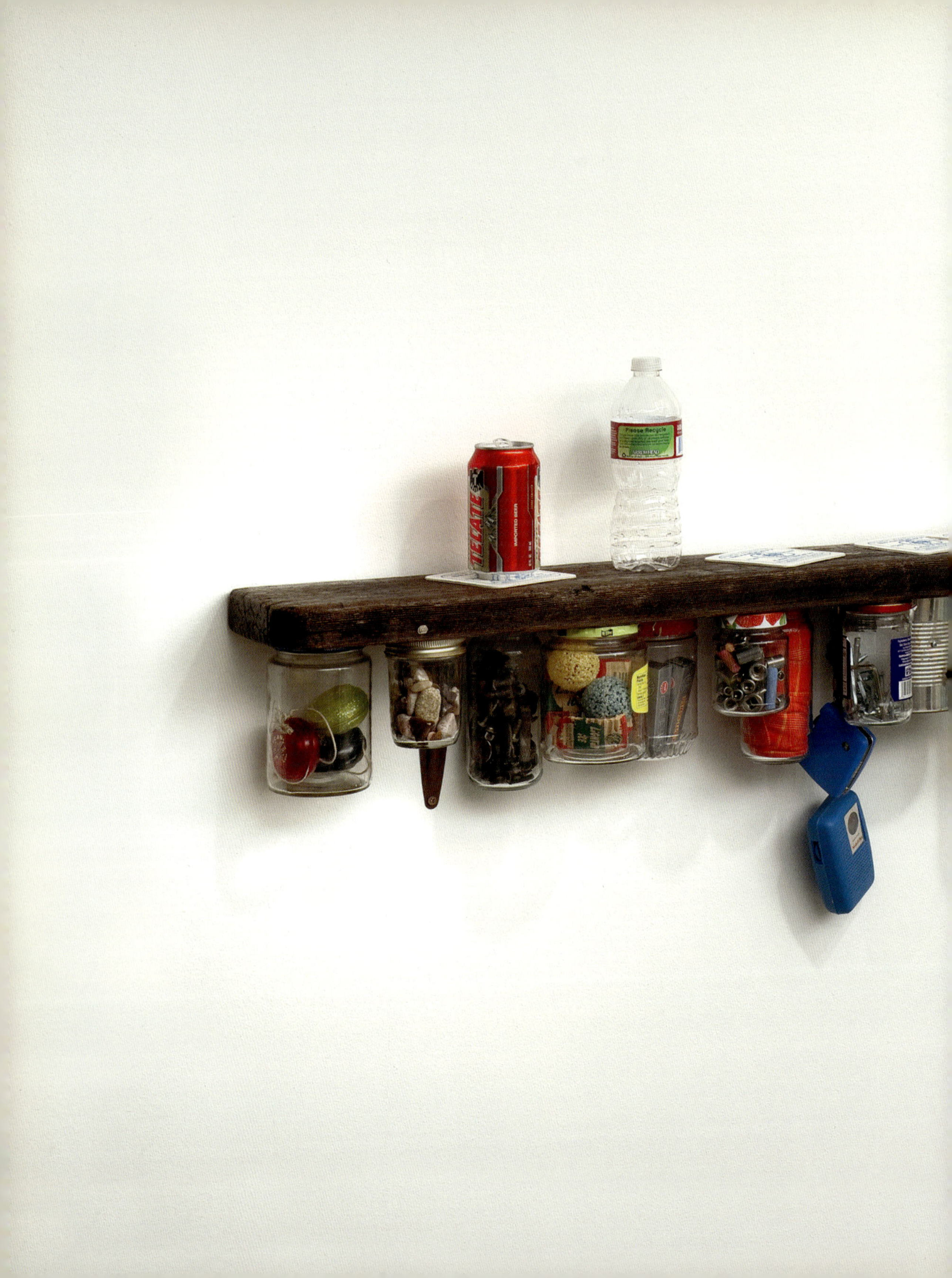
Please Recycle
TECATE
IMPORTED BEER

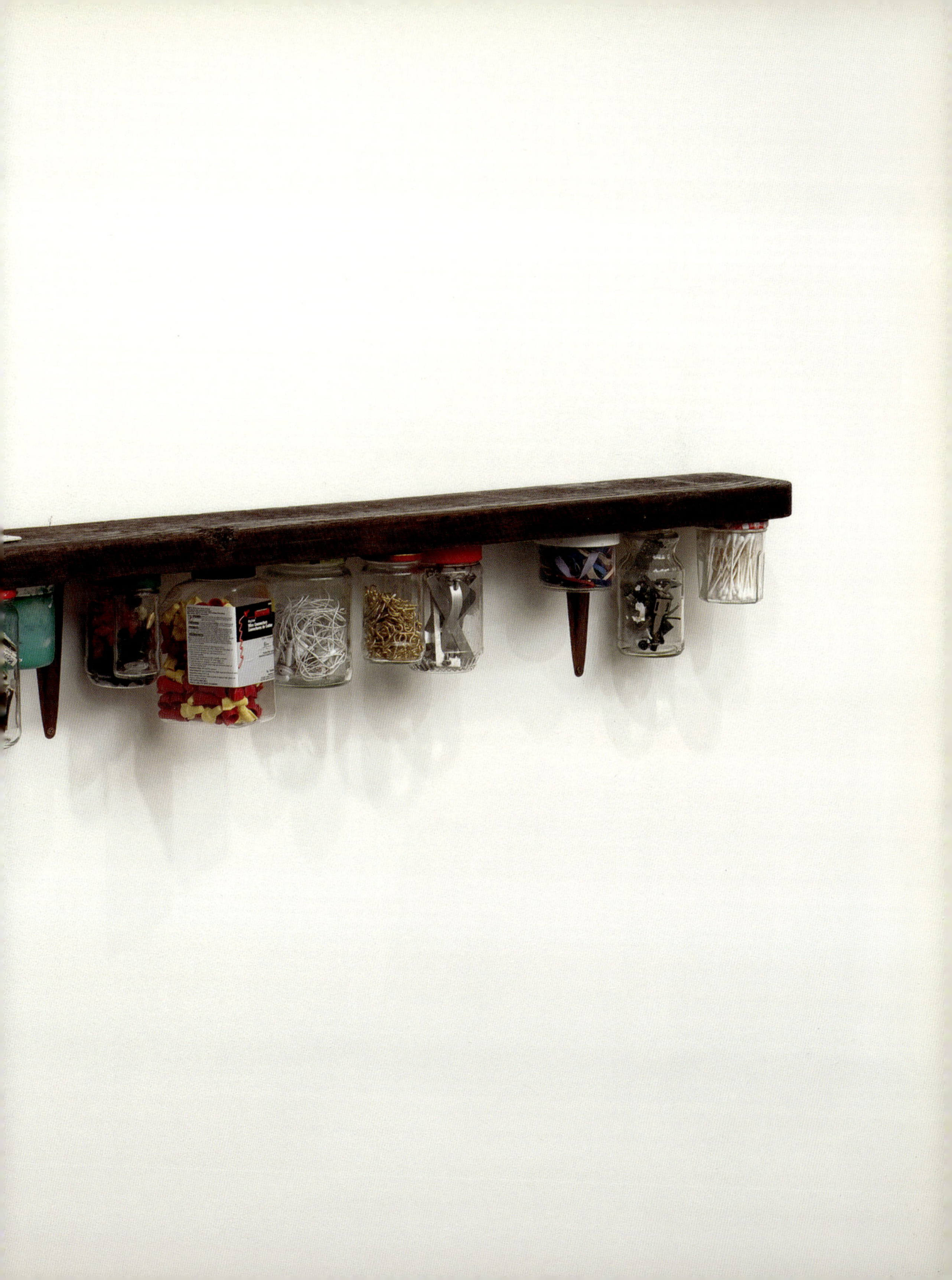

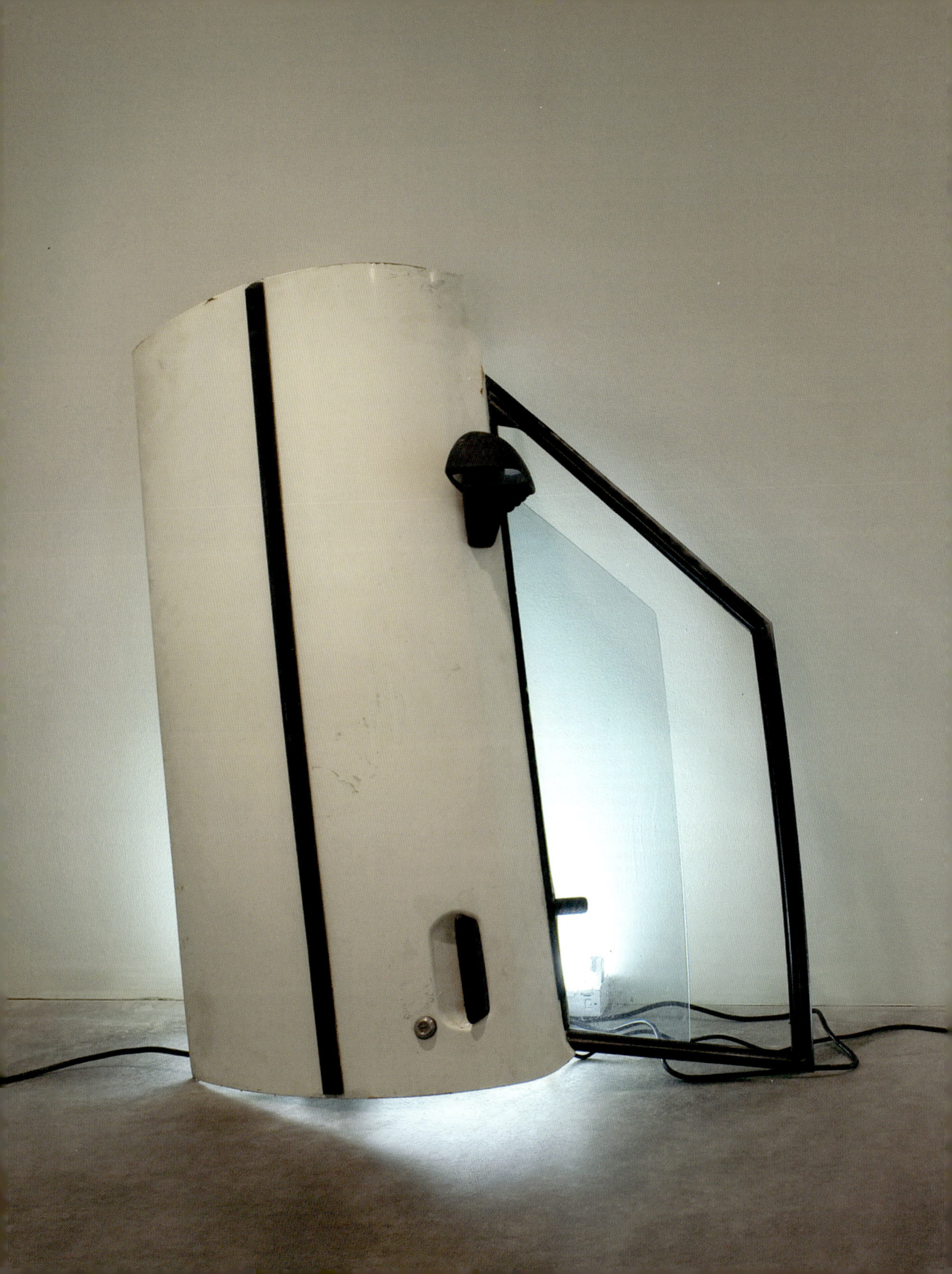

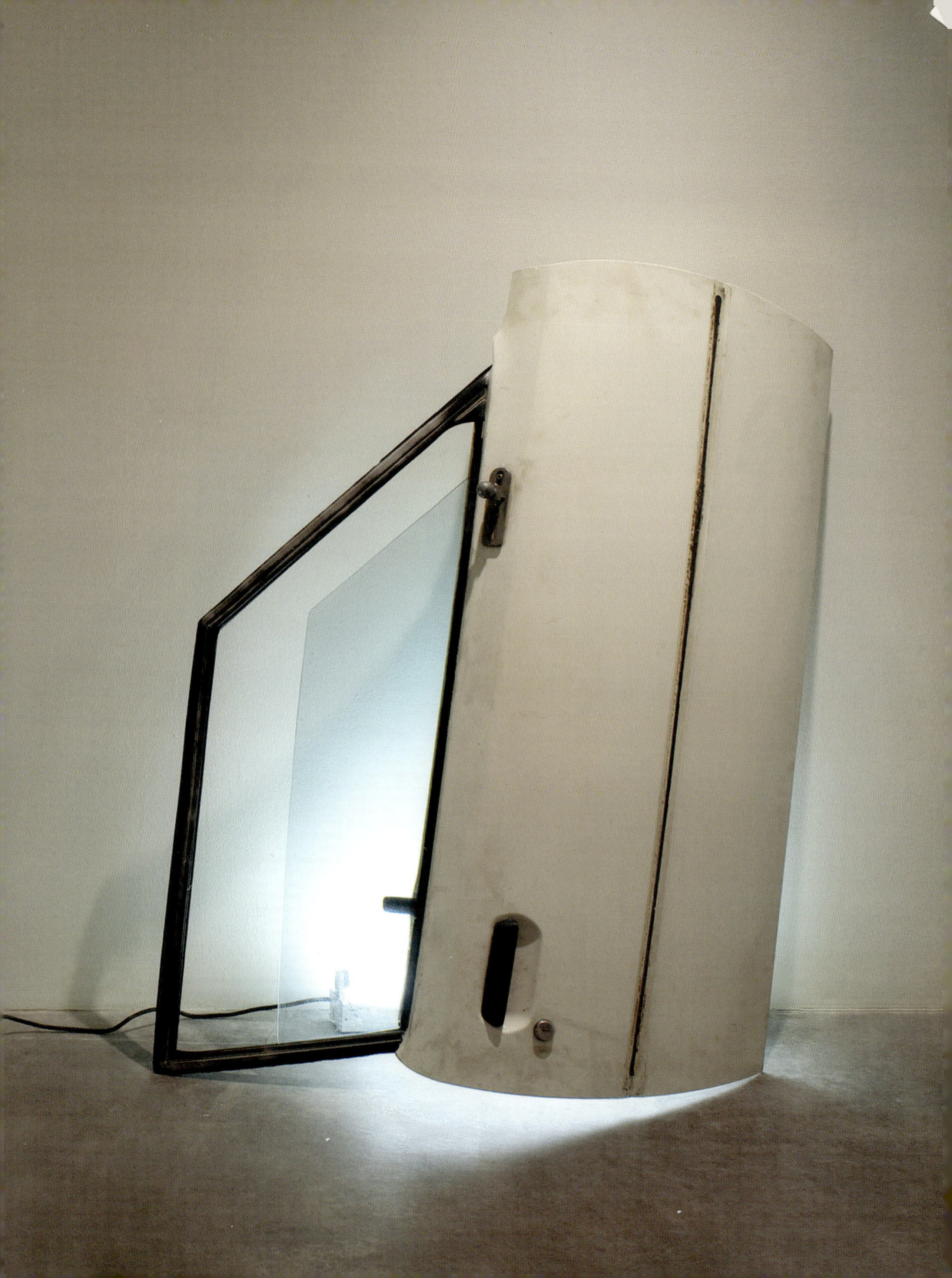

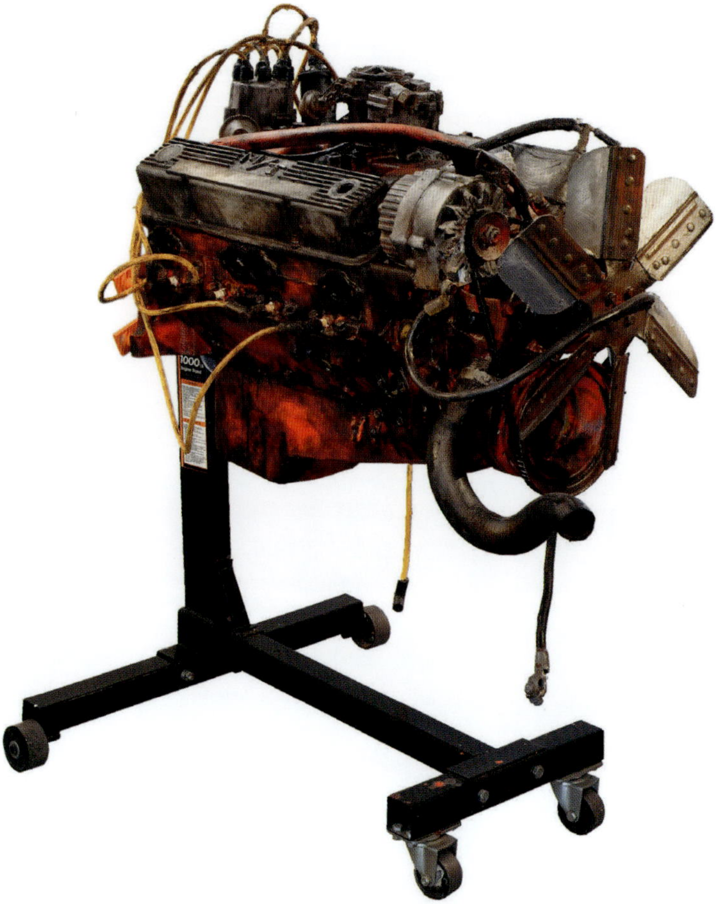

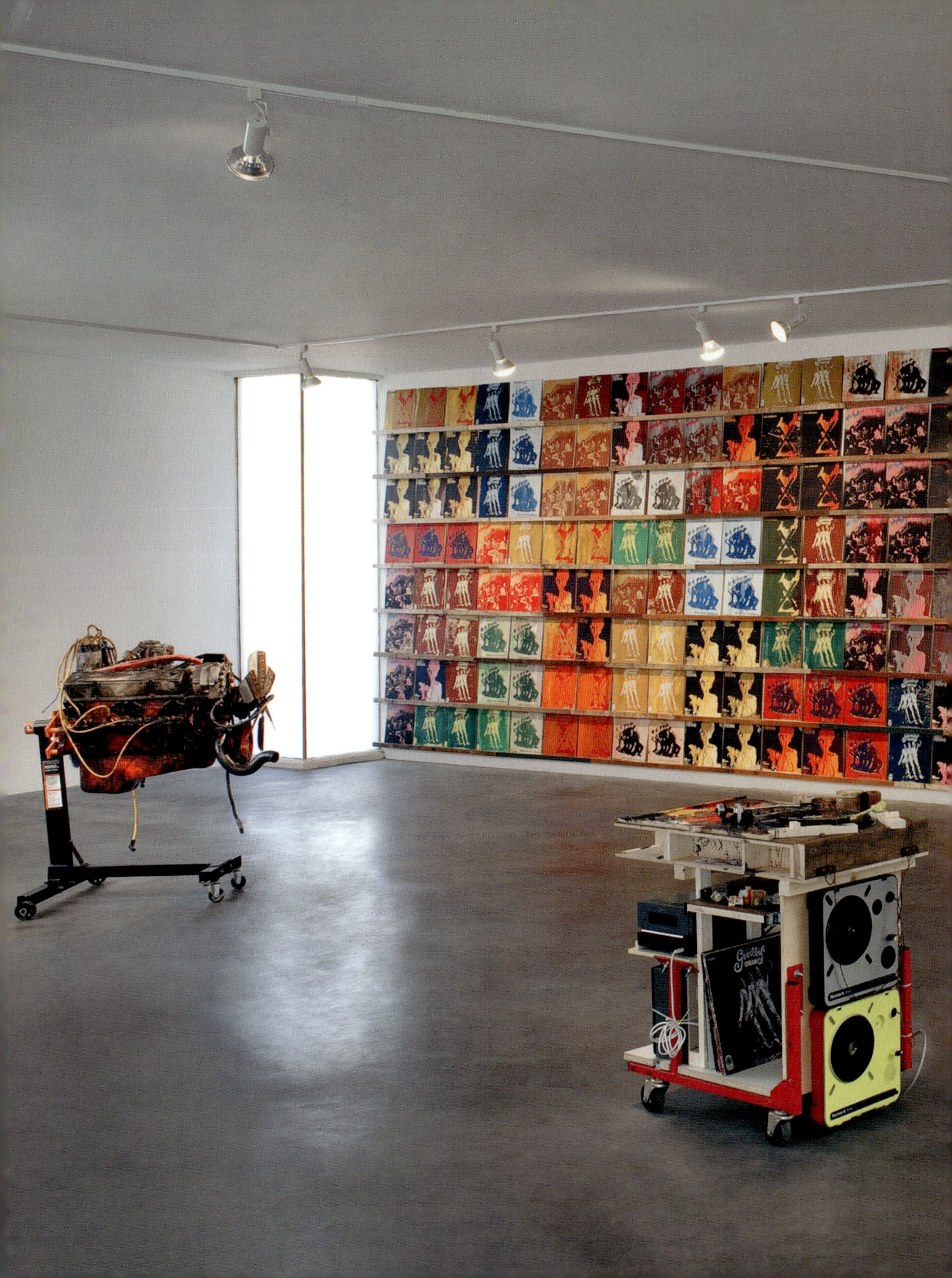

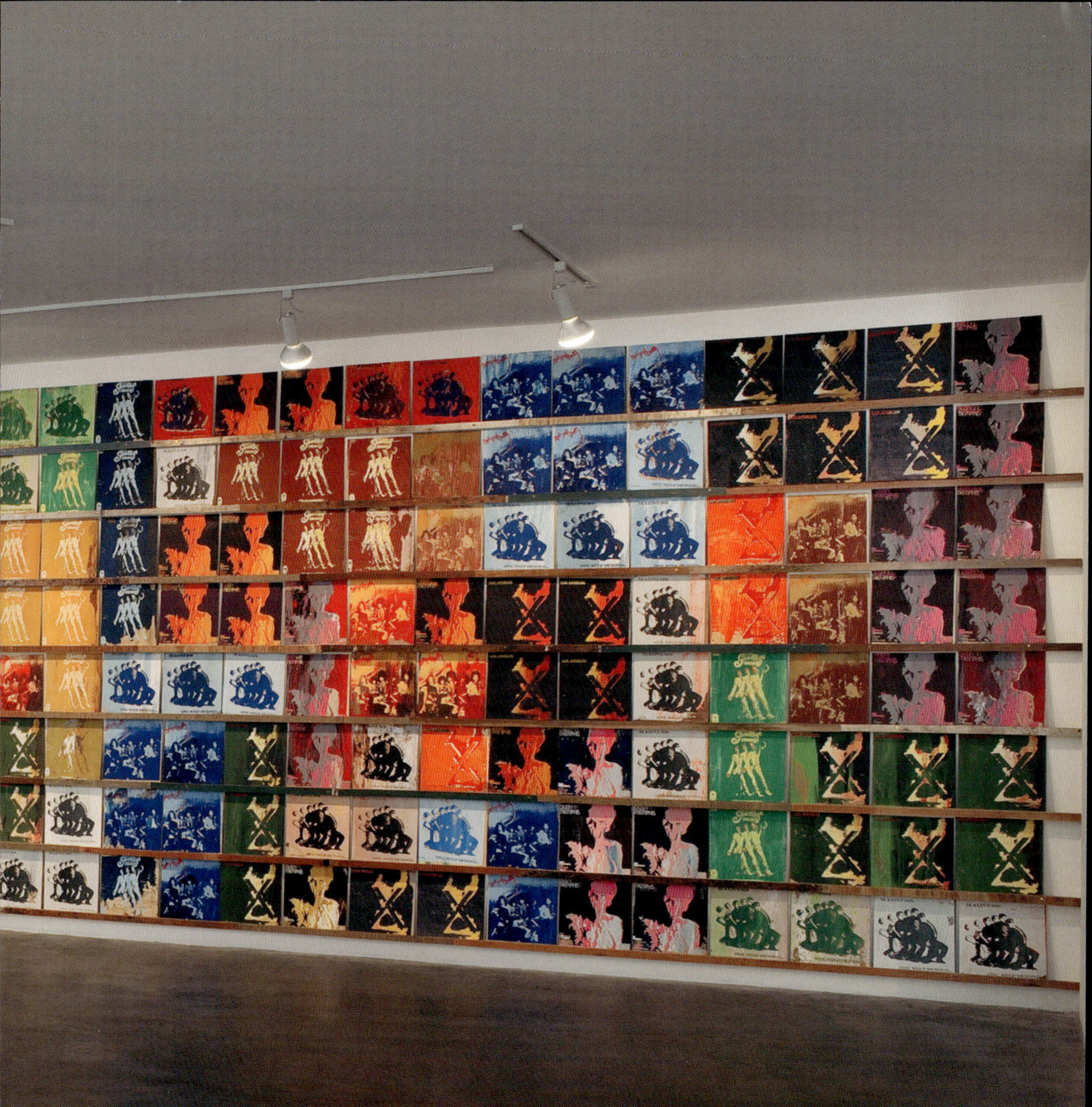

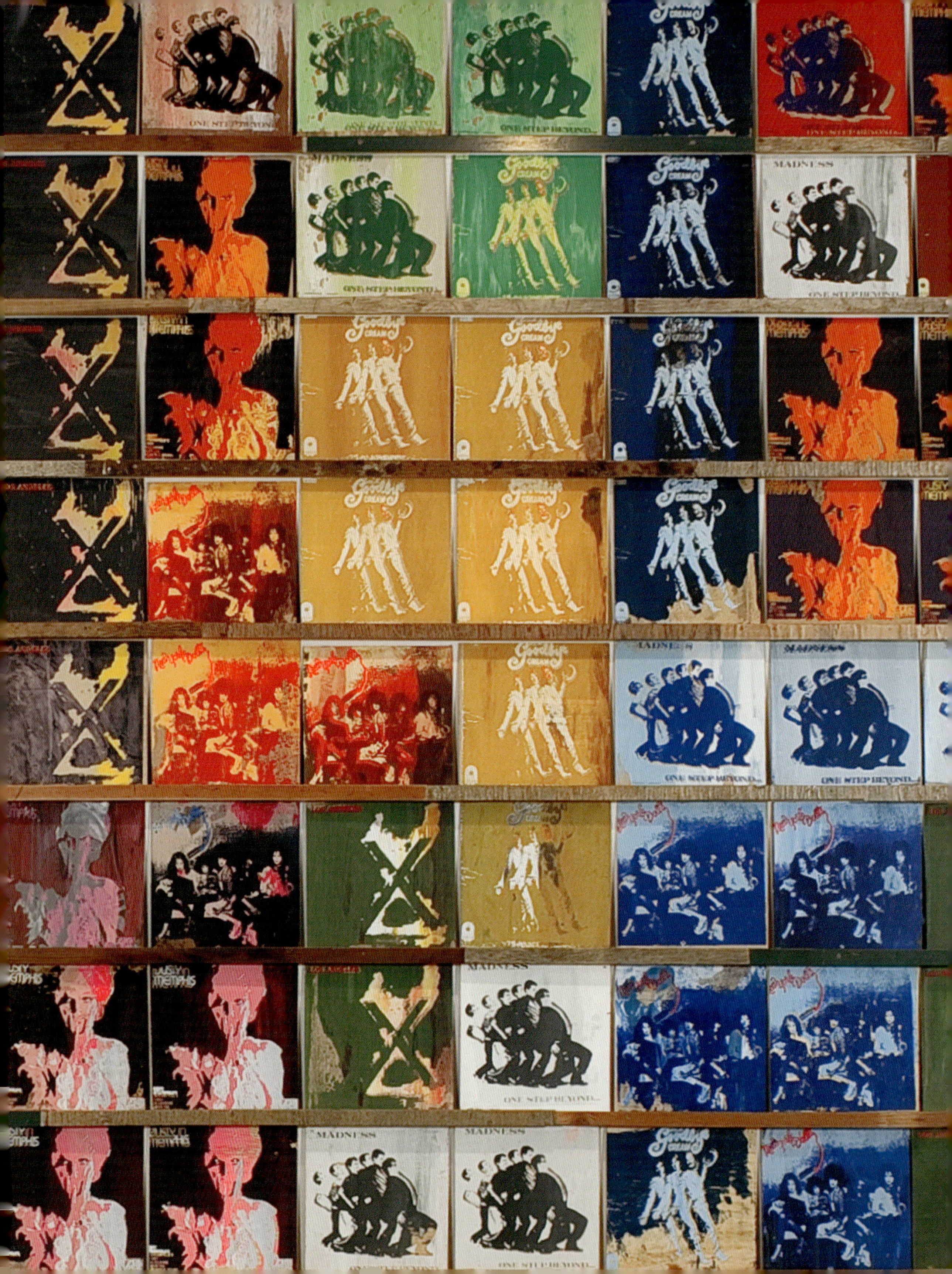
ONE STEP BEYOND...
MADNESS
Goodbye
CREAM
MEMPHIS

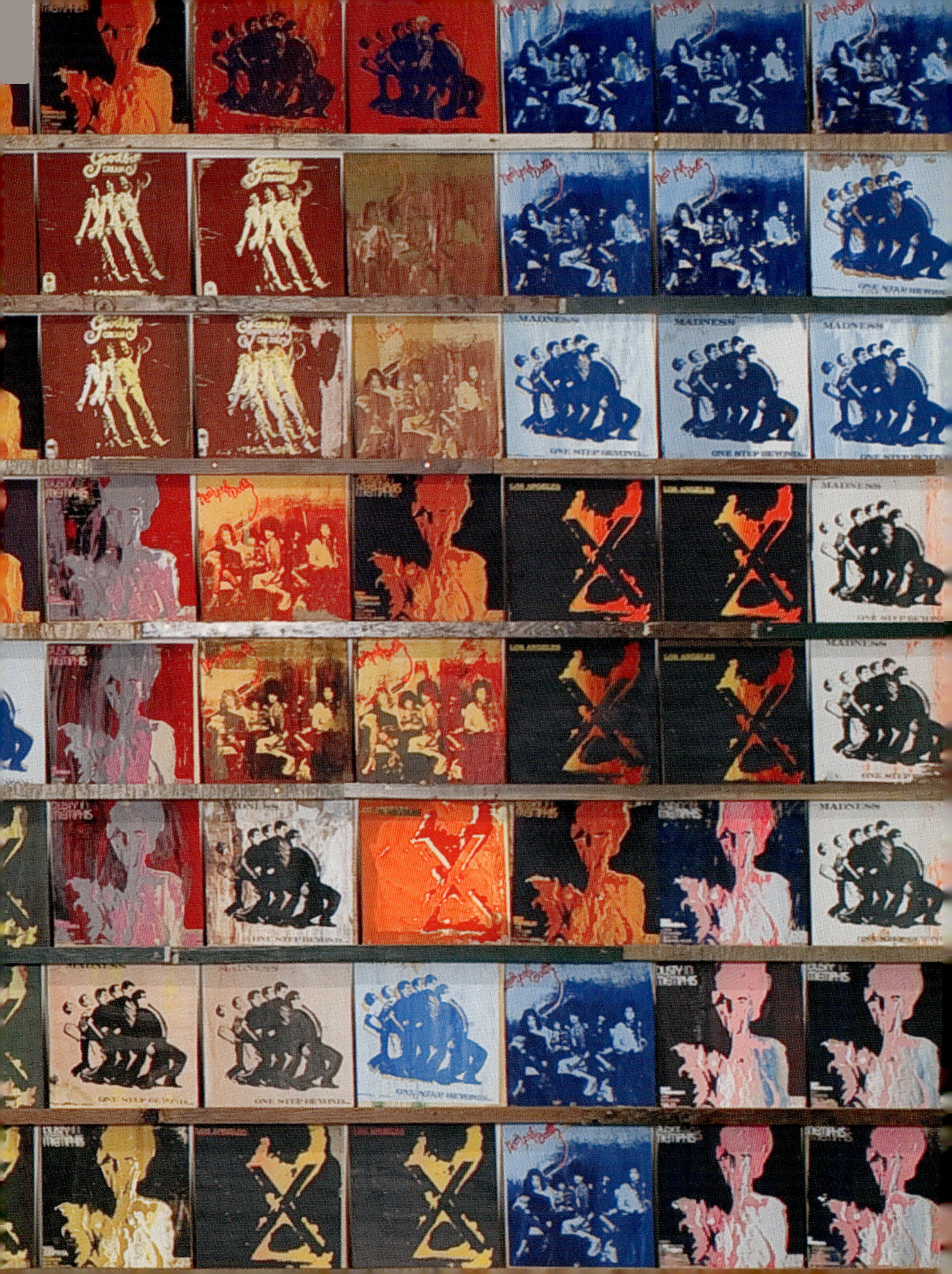
MADNESS
ONE STEP BEYOND...
LOS ANGELES

SEAN
DUFFY

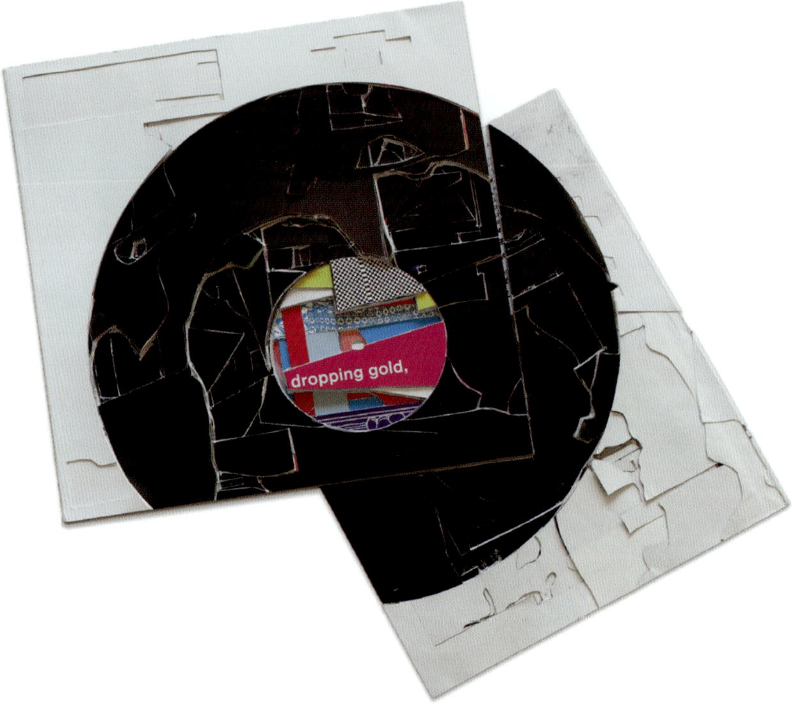
dropping gold,

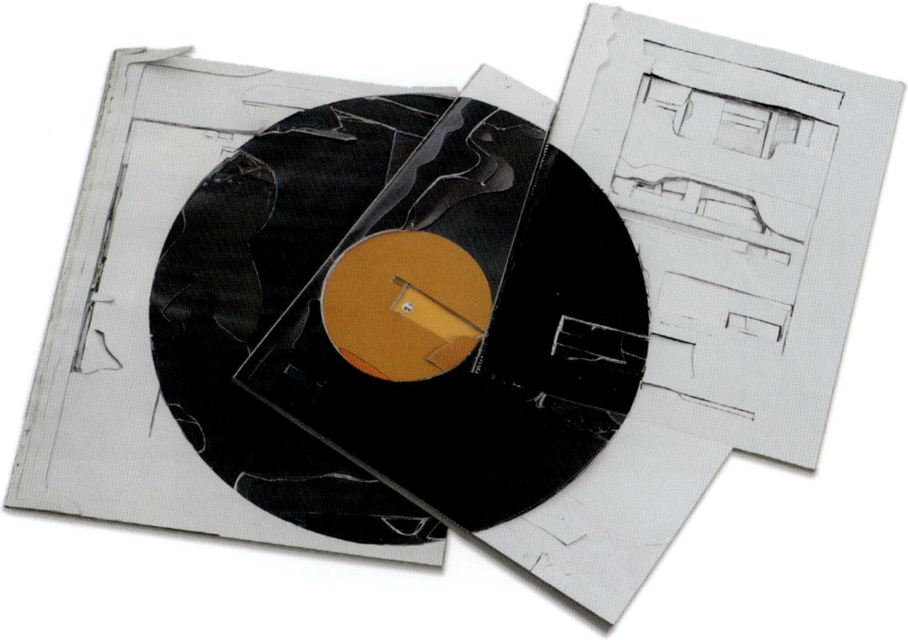

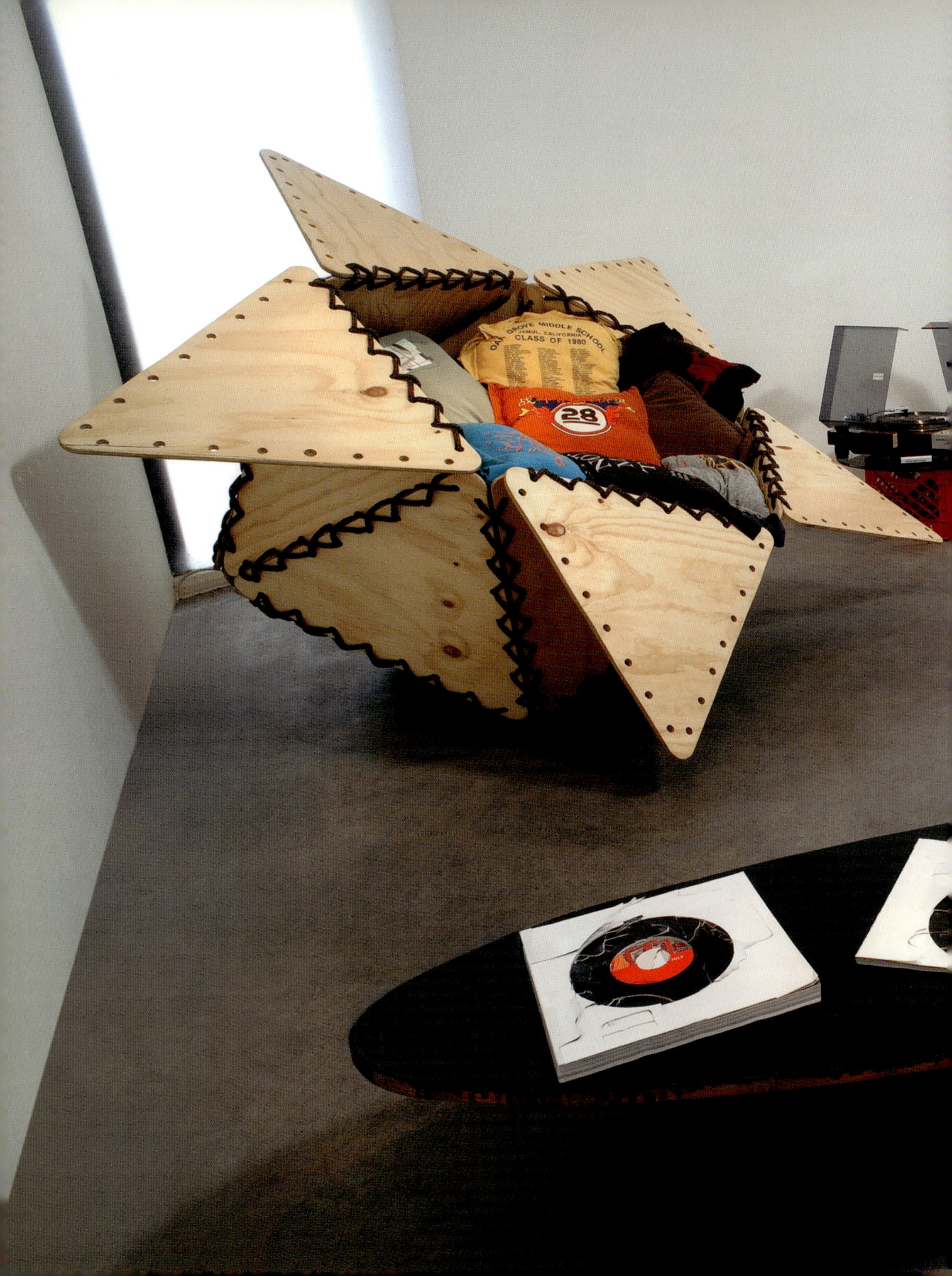
GROVE MIDDLE SCHOOL
JAMUL, CALIFORNIA
CLASS OF 1980
28

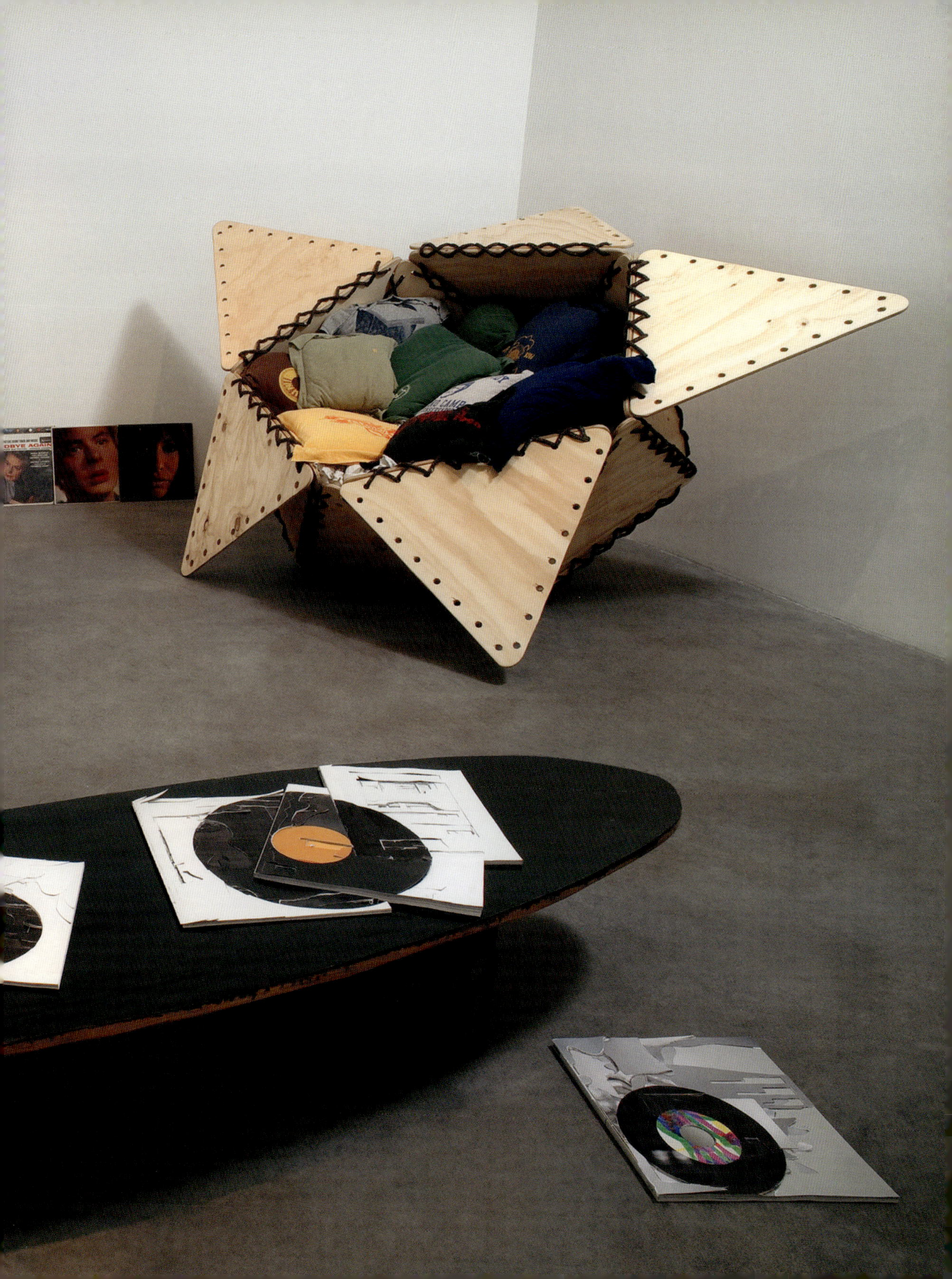

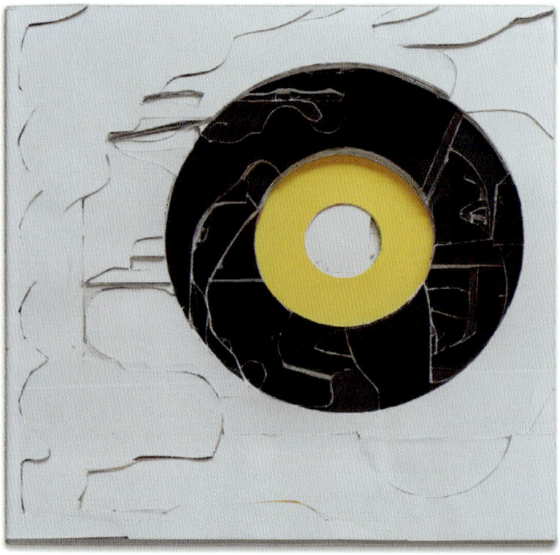

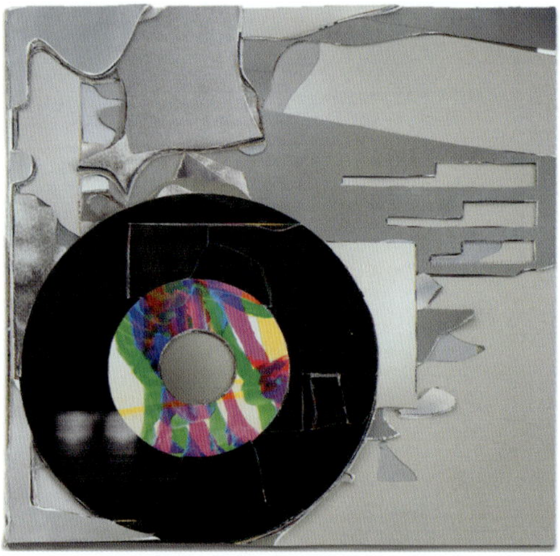

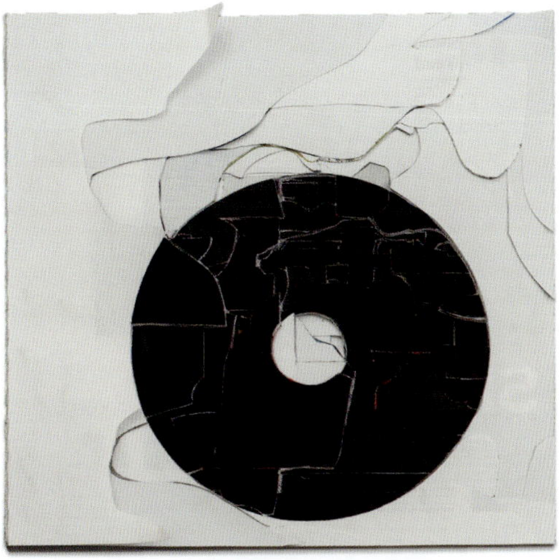

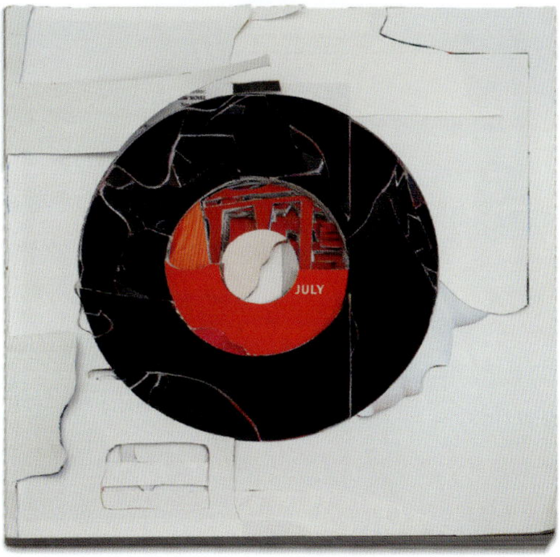
JULY

SEAN DUFFY

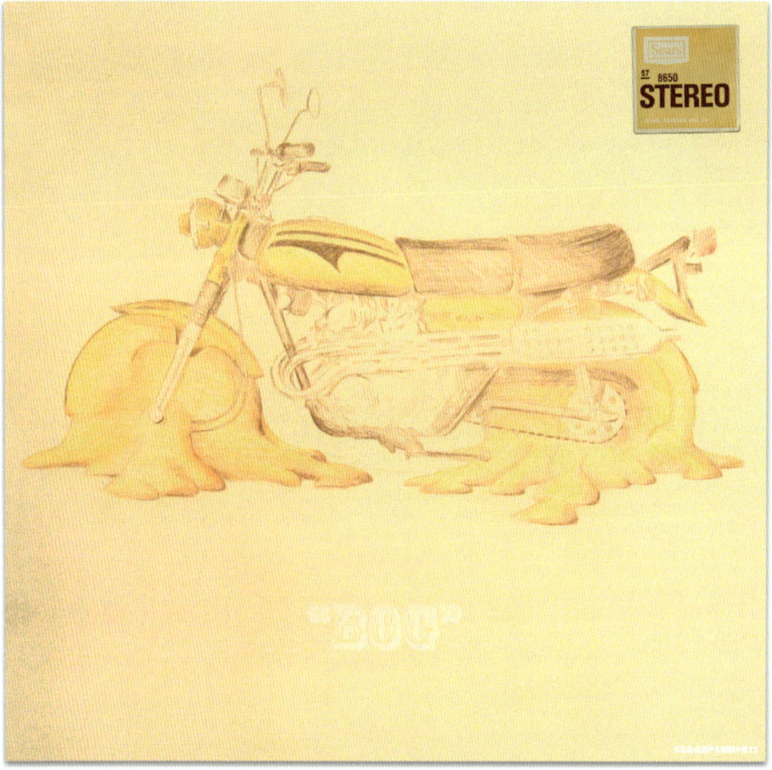
Sears
57 8650
STEREO

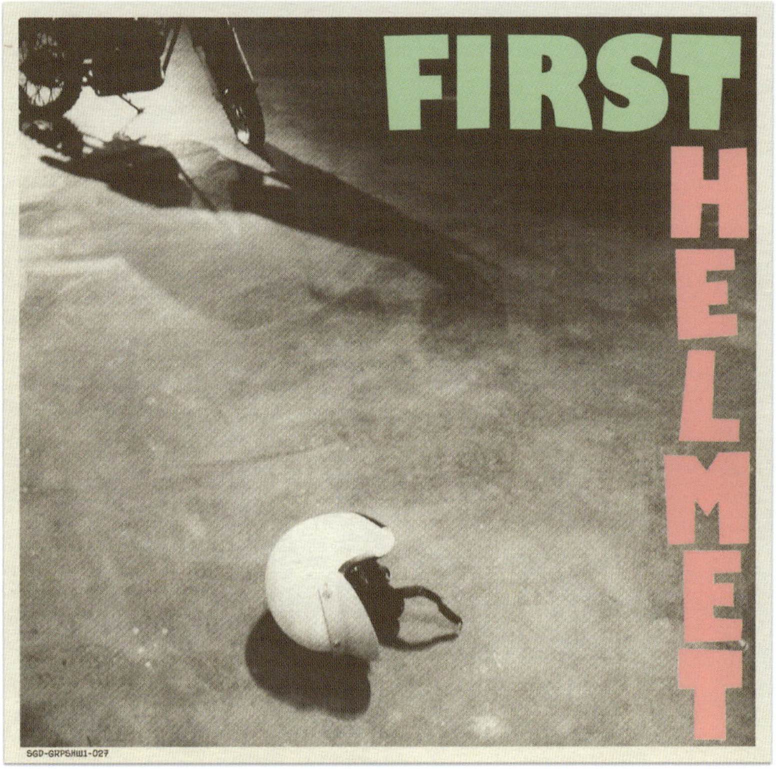
FIRST
HELMET
SGD-GRPSHW1-027

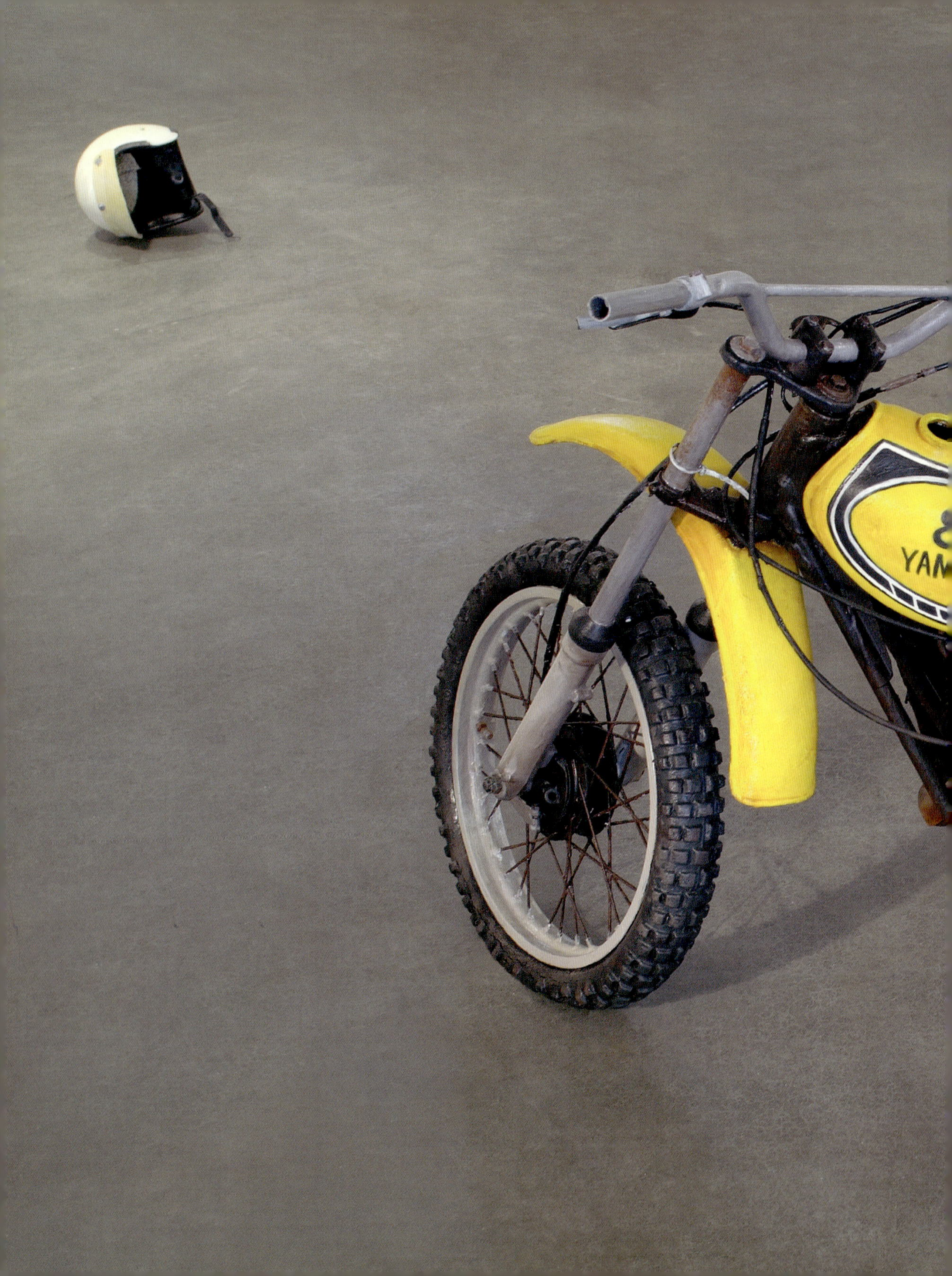

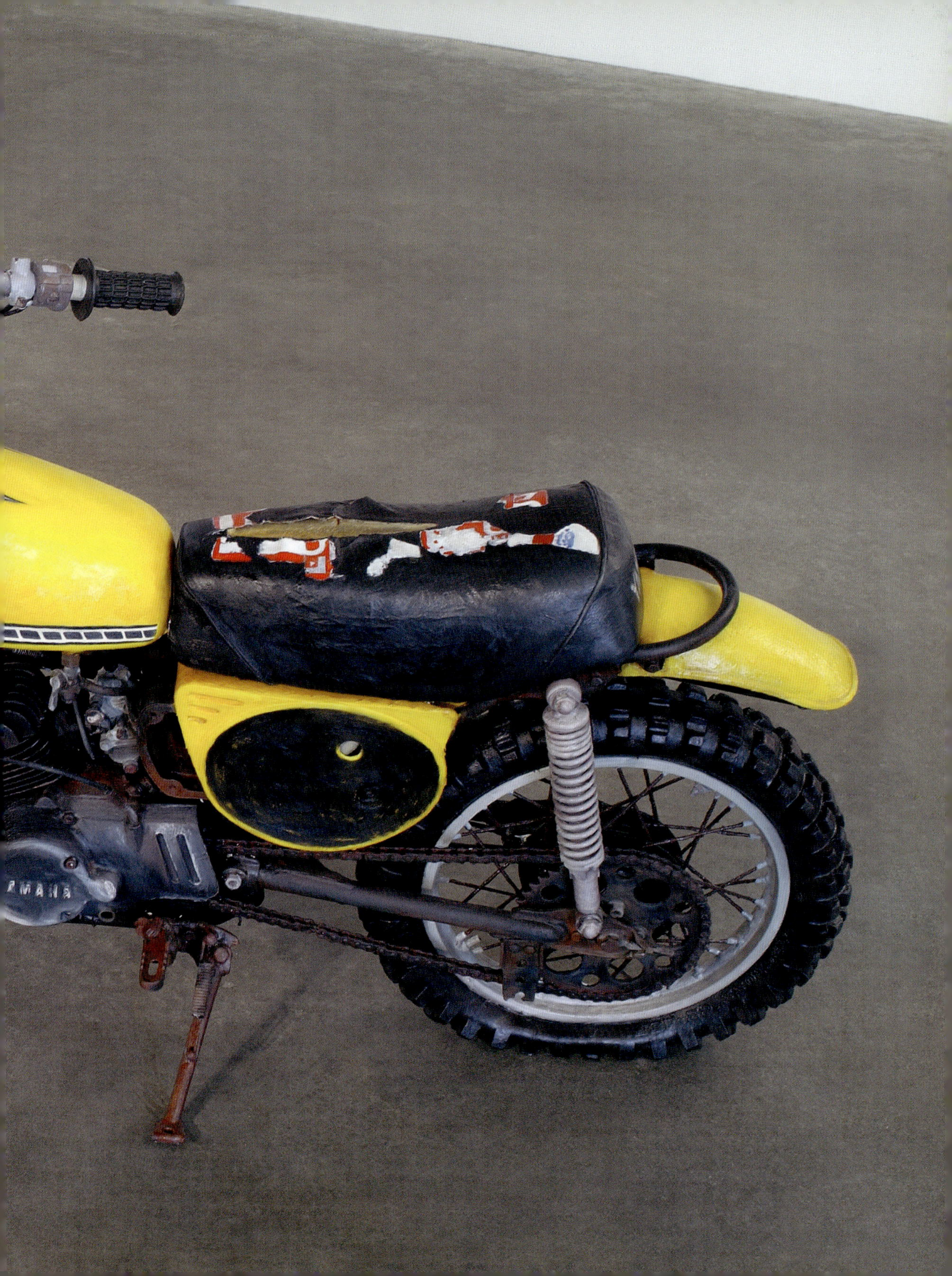

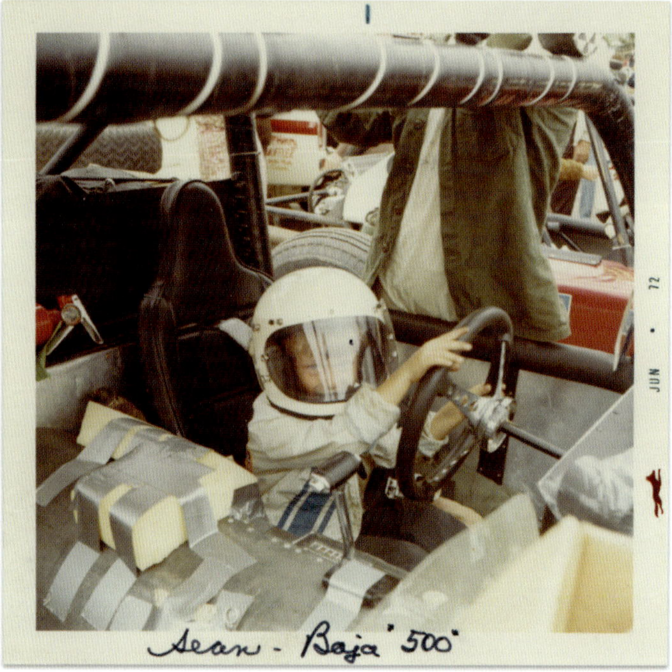
JUN • 72
Sean - Baja '500'

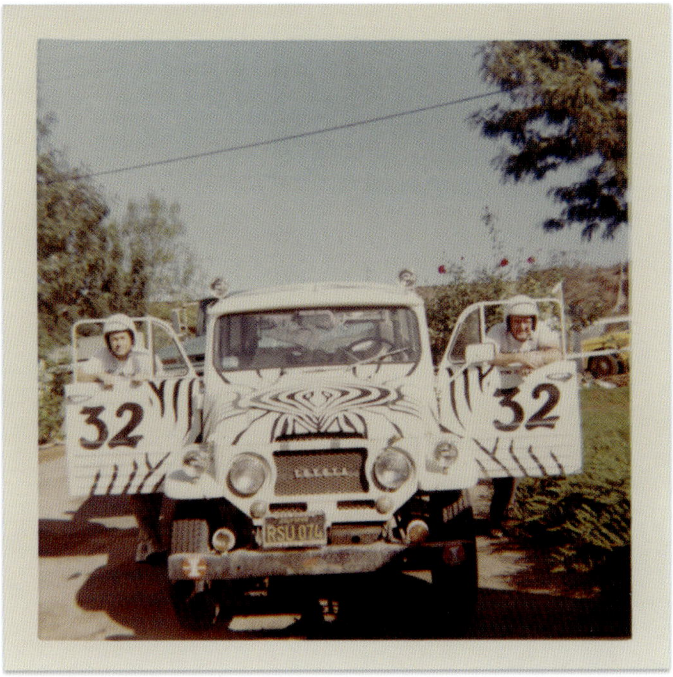
32
32

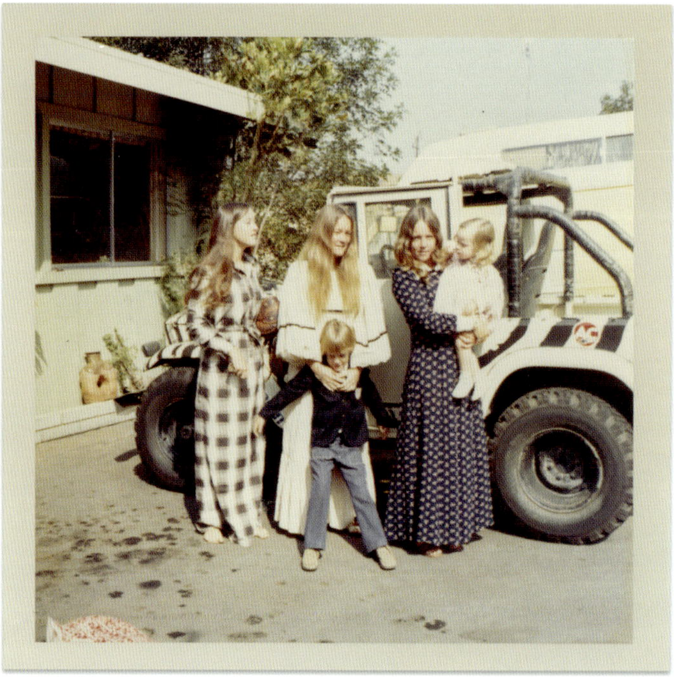

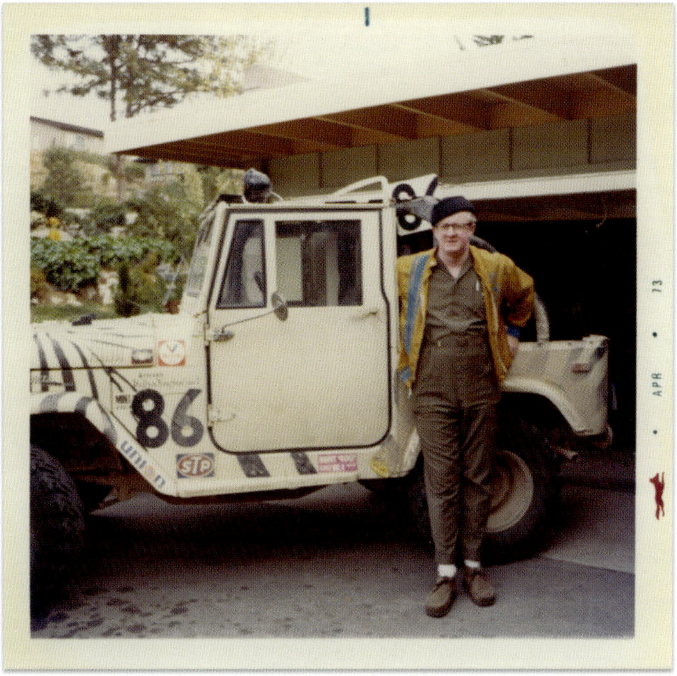
86
STP

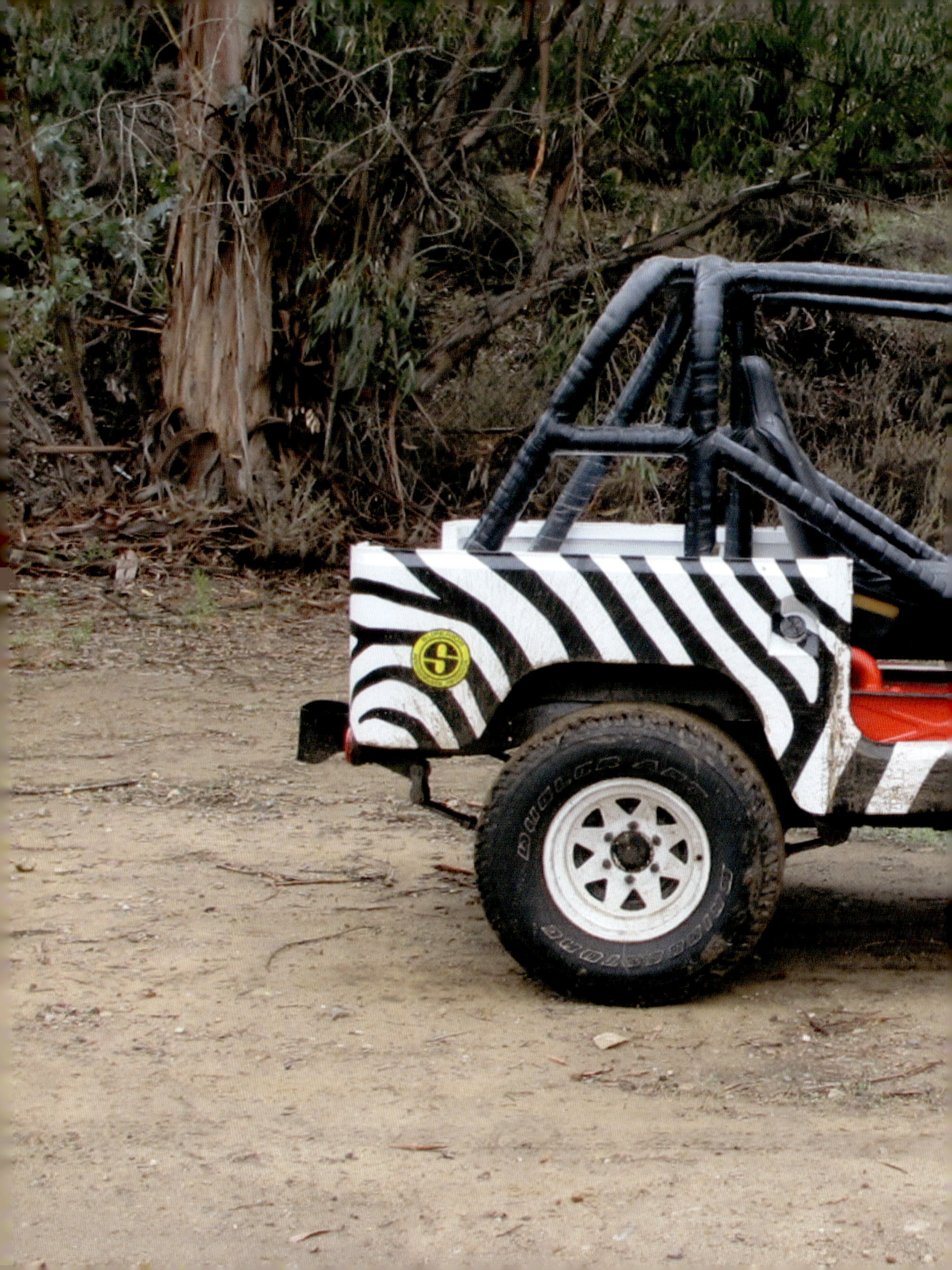

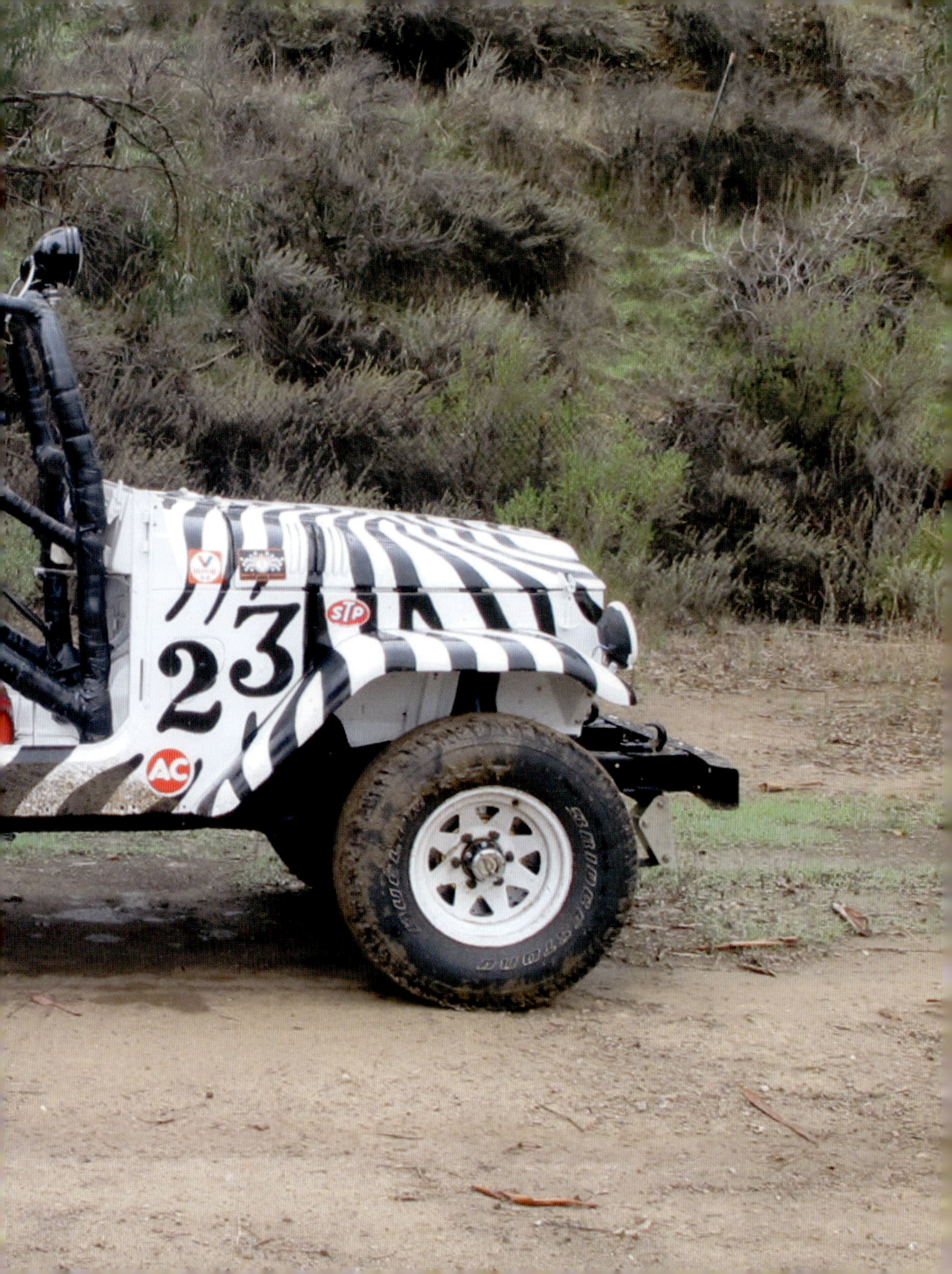
23
STP
AC

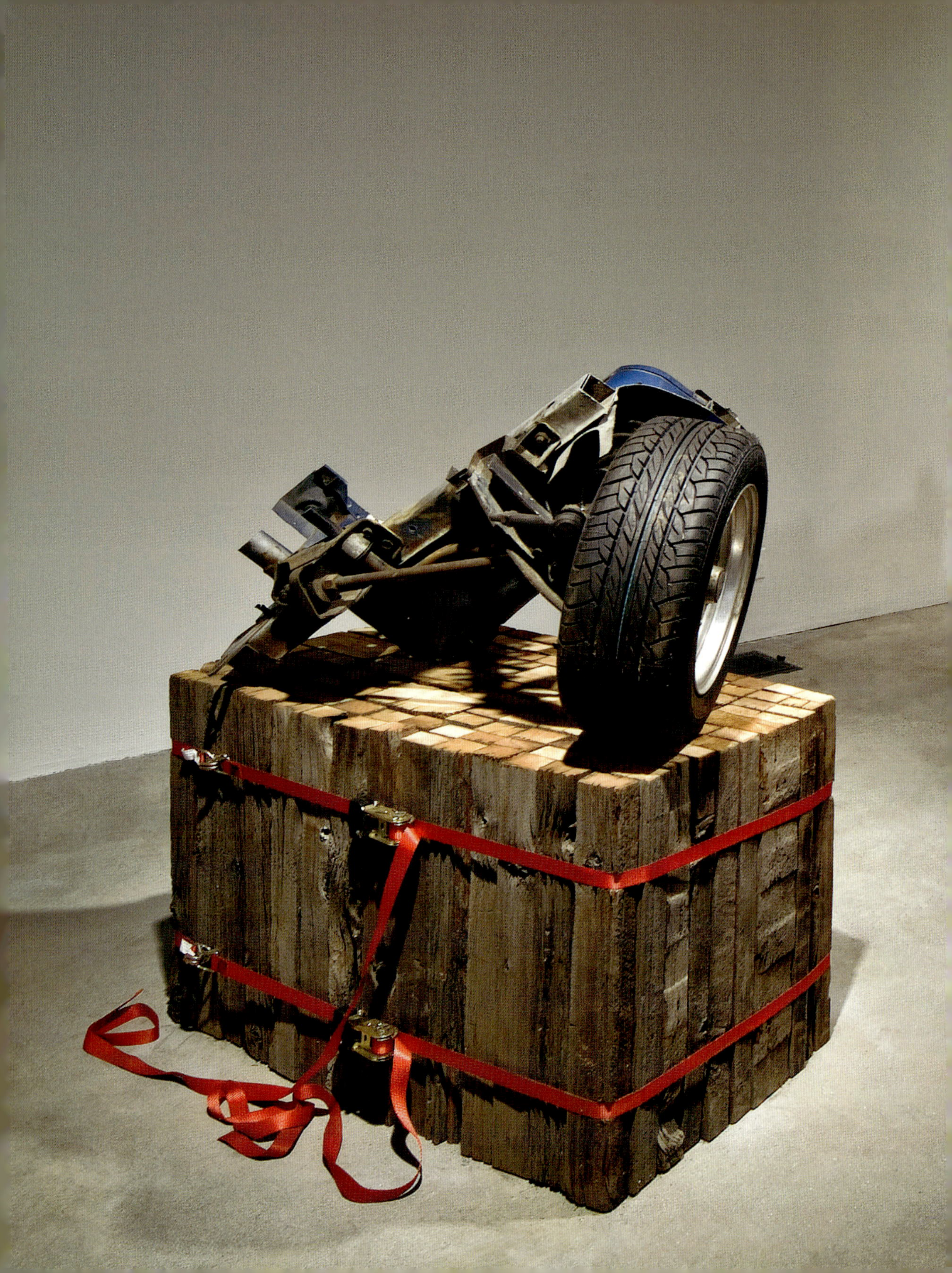

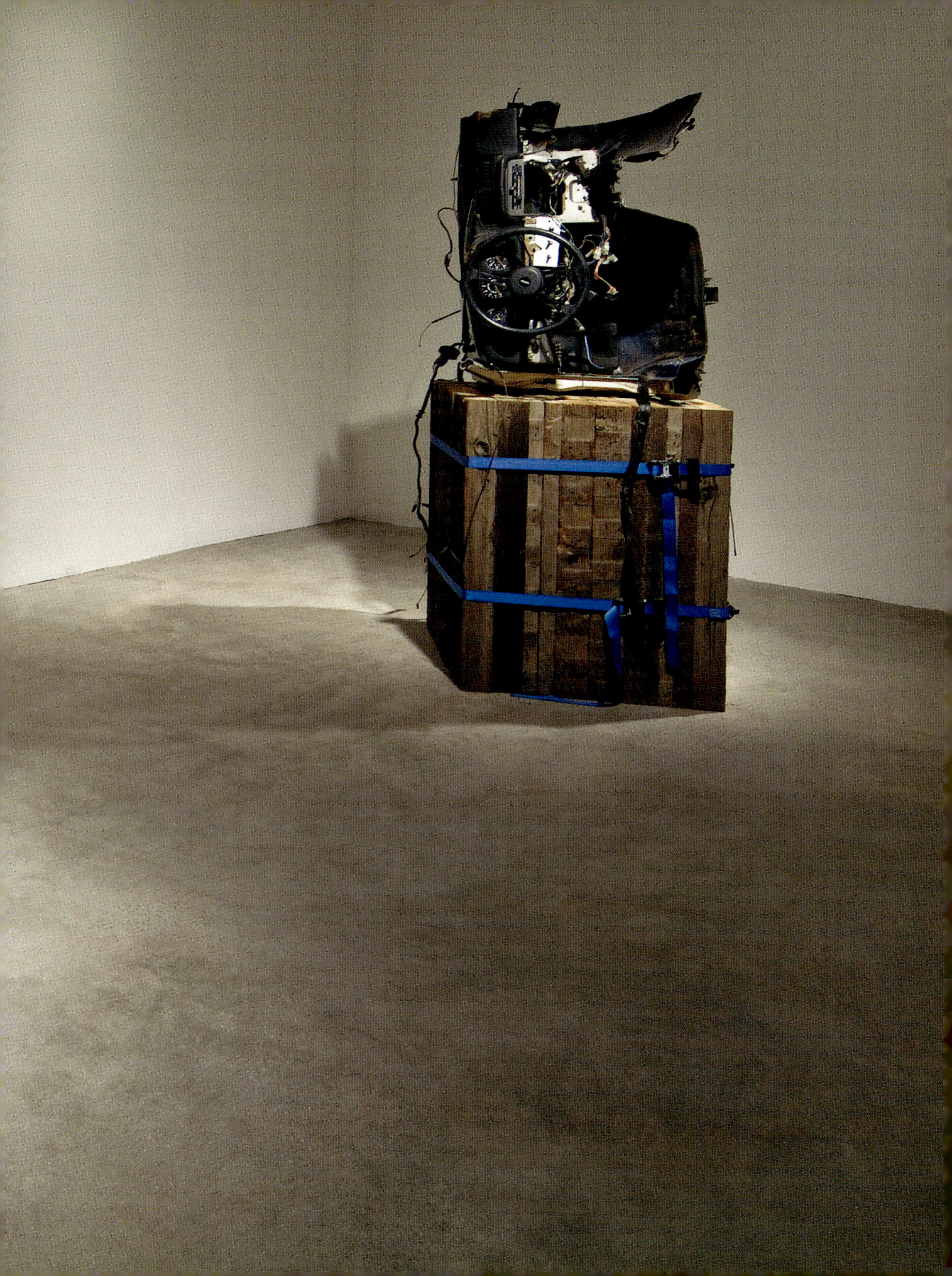

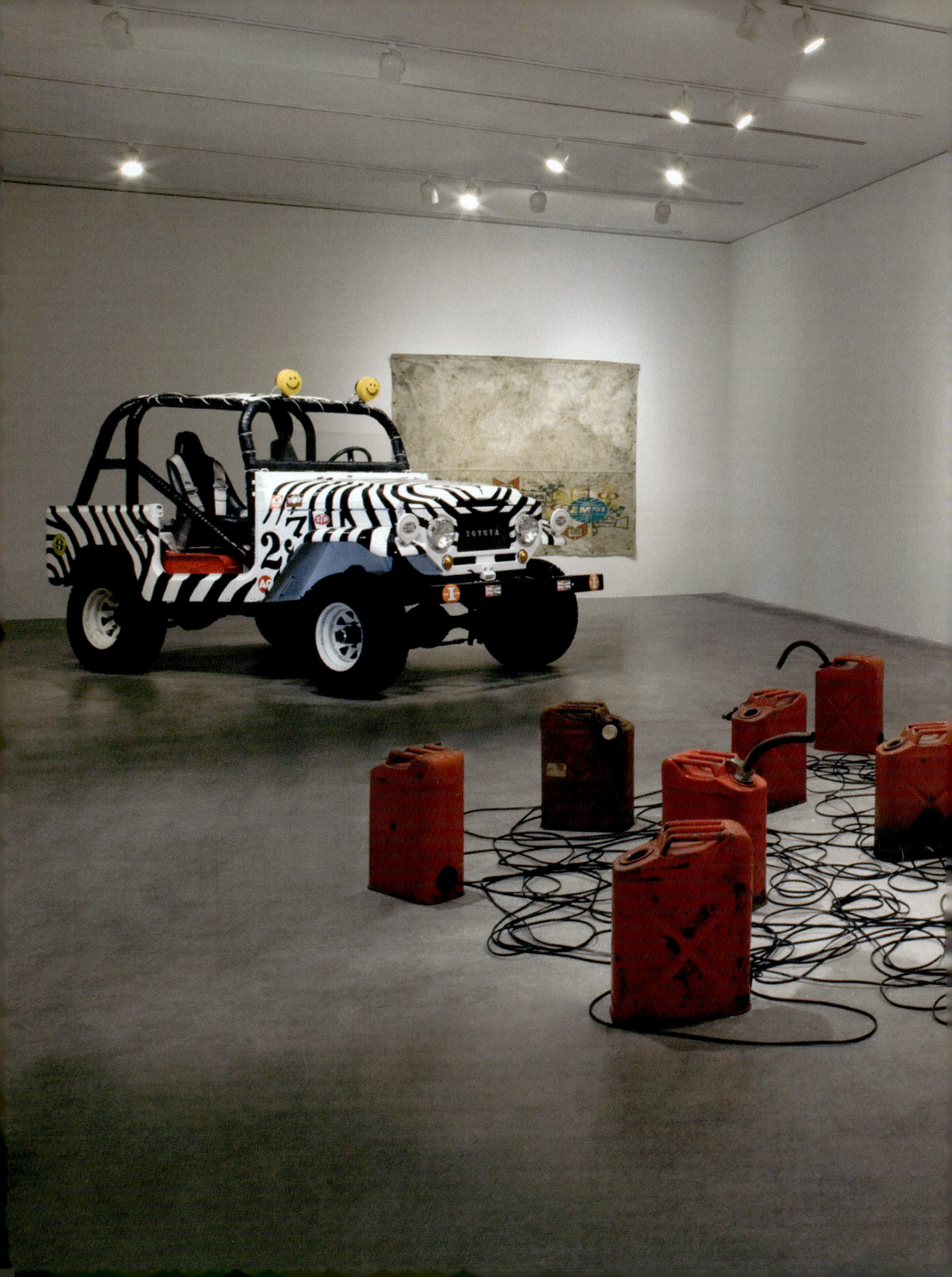
TOYOTA

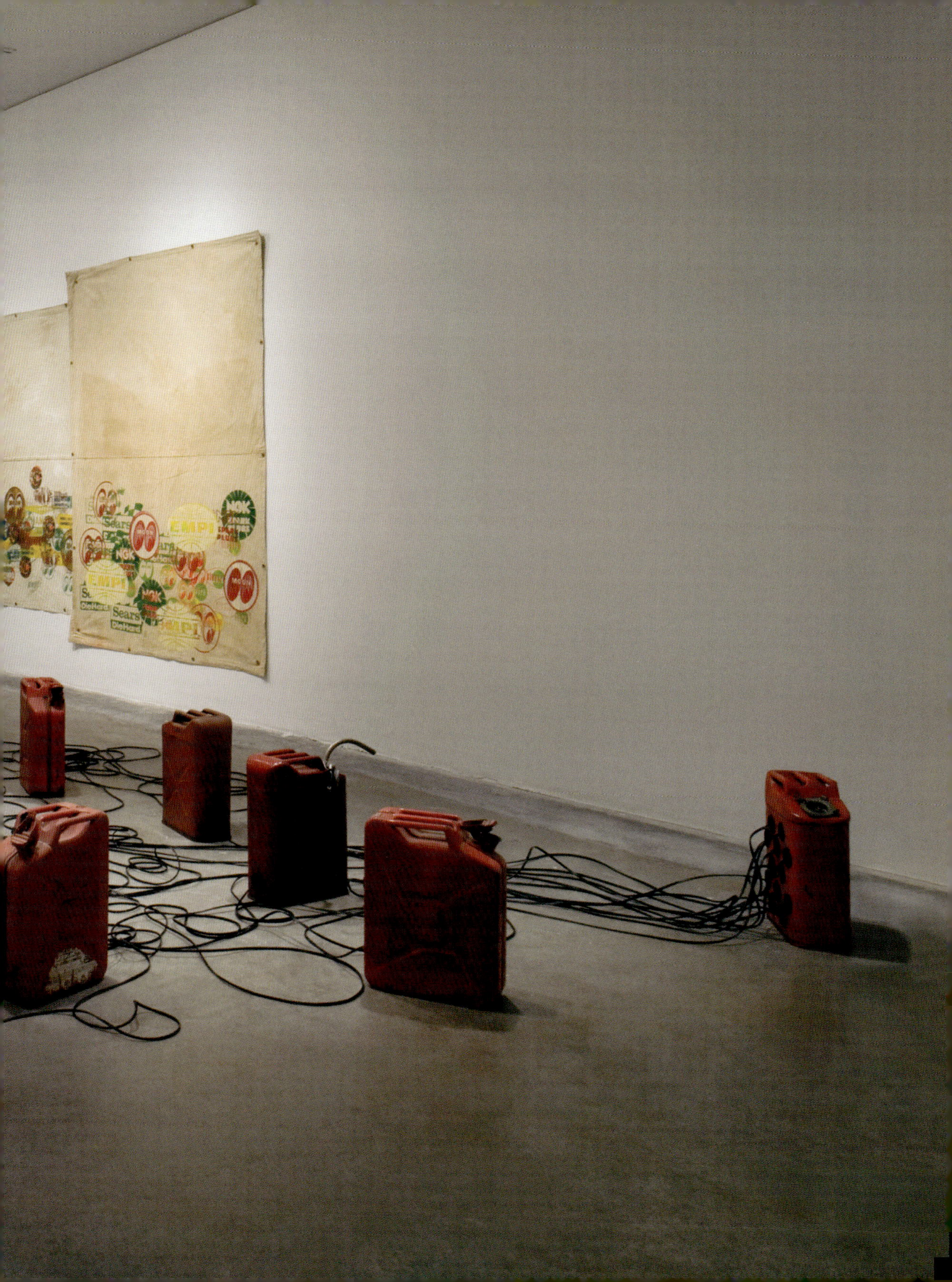
Sears
EMPI

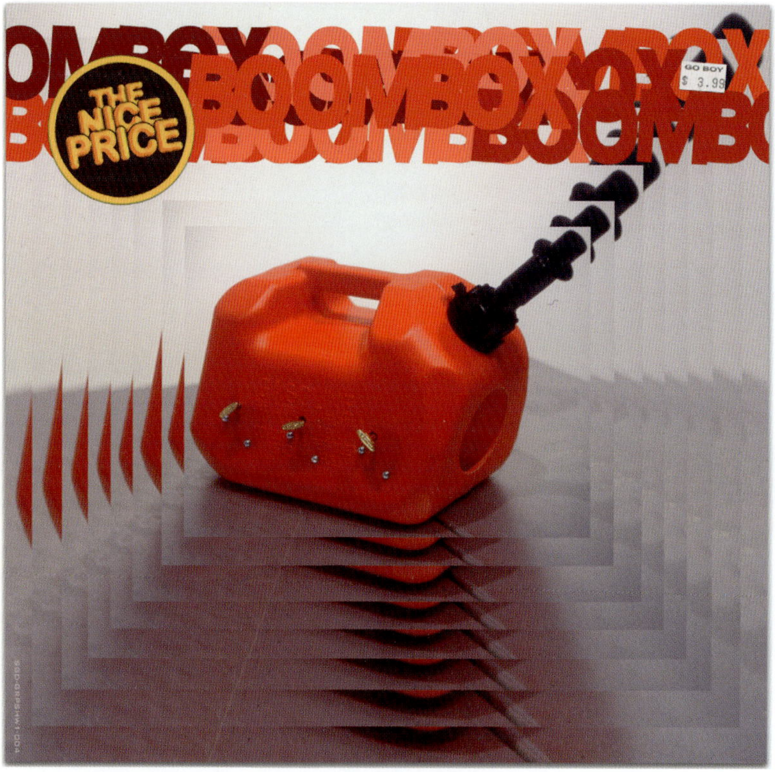
BOOMBOX
THE NICE PRICE
GO BOY
$ 3.99

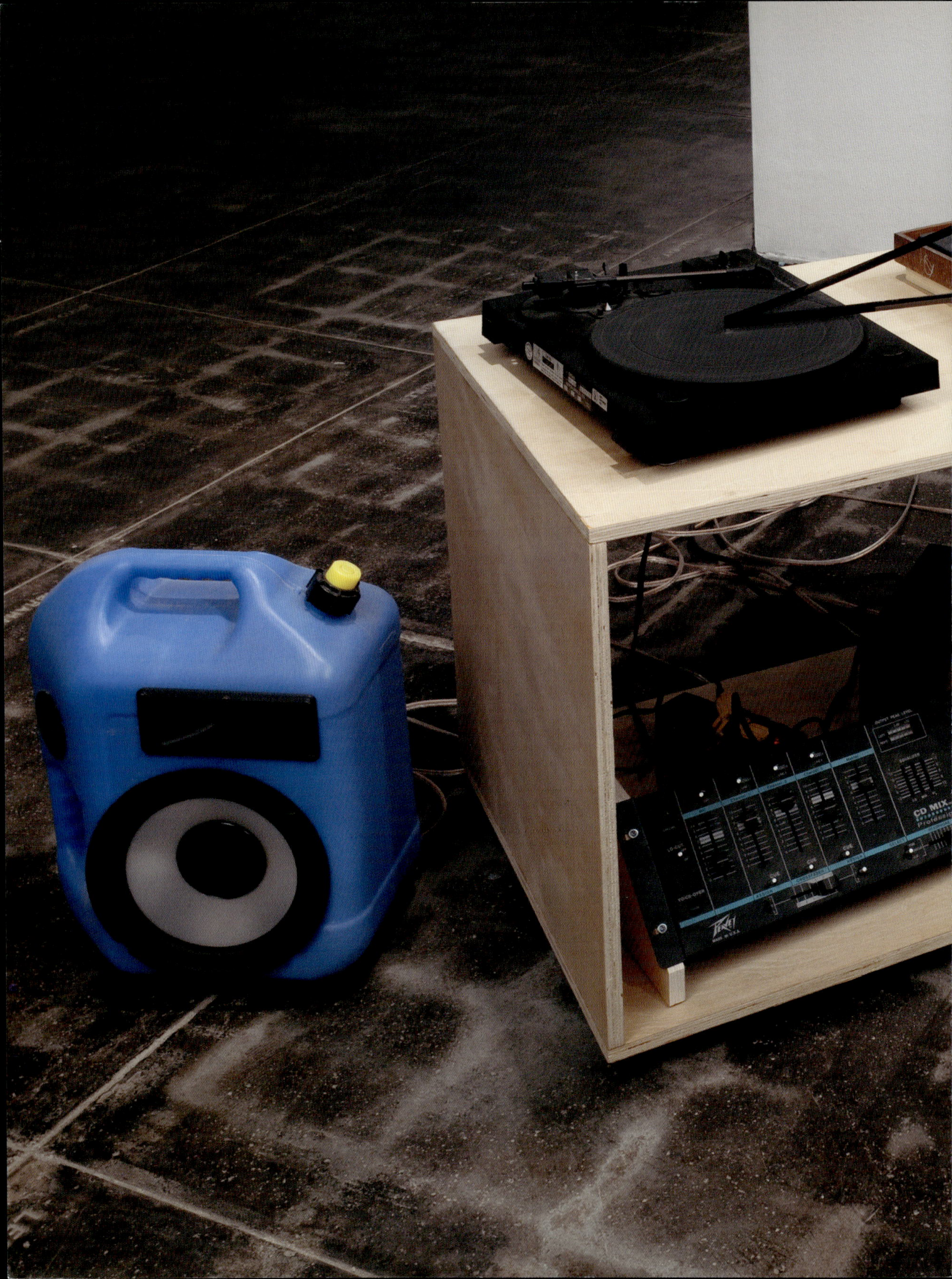
CD MIX

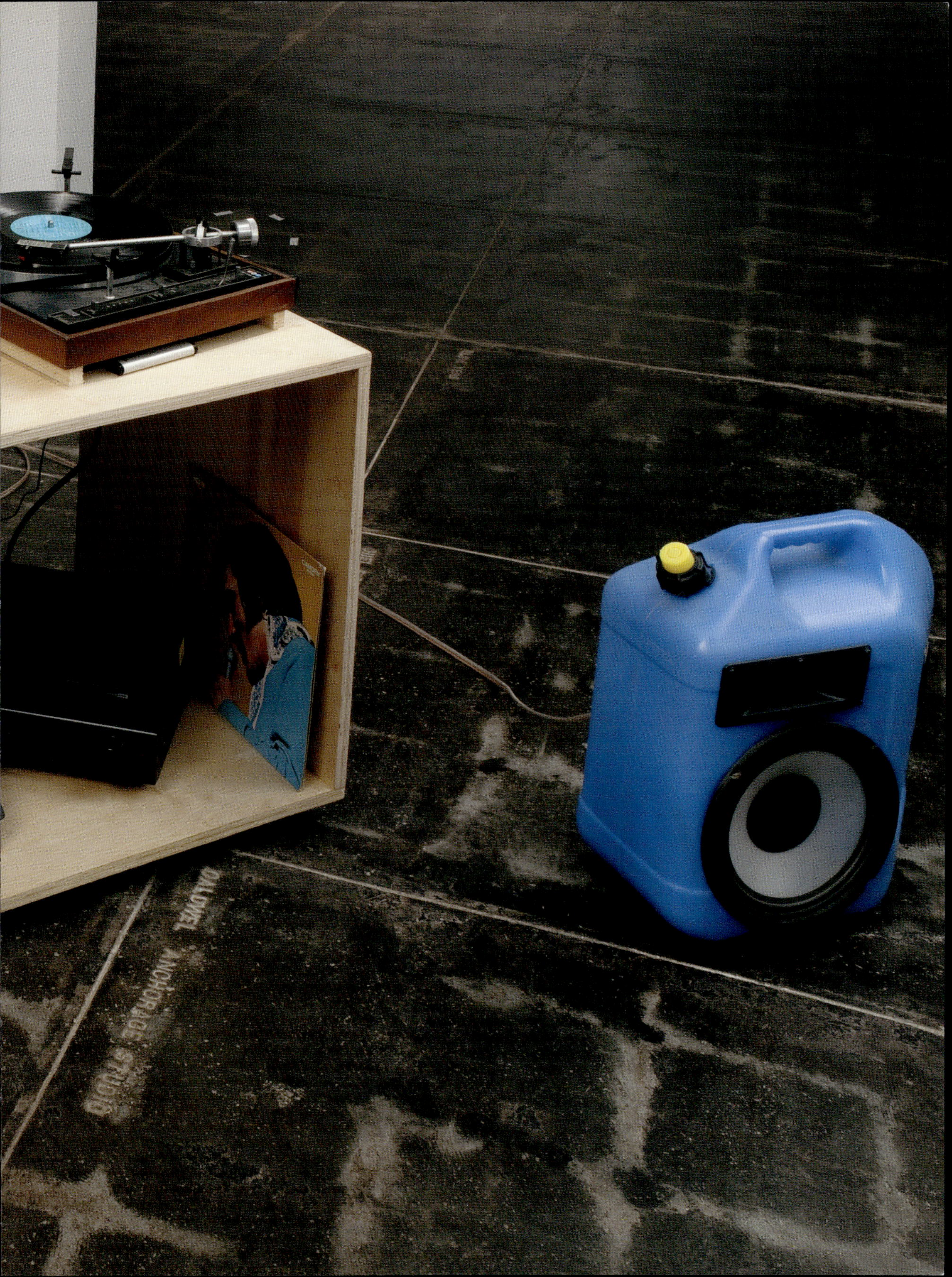

SEAN

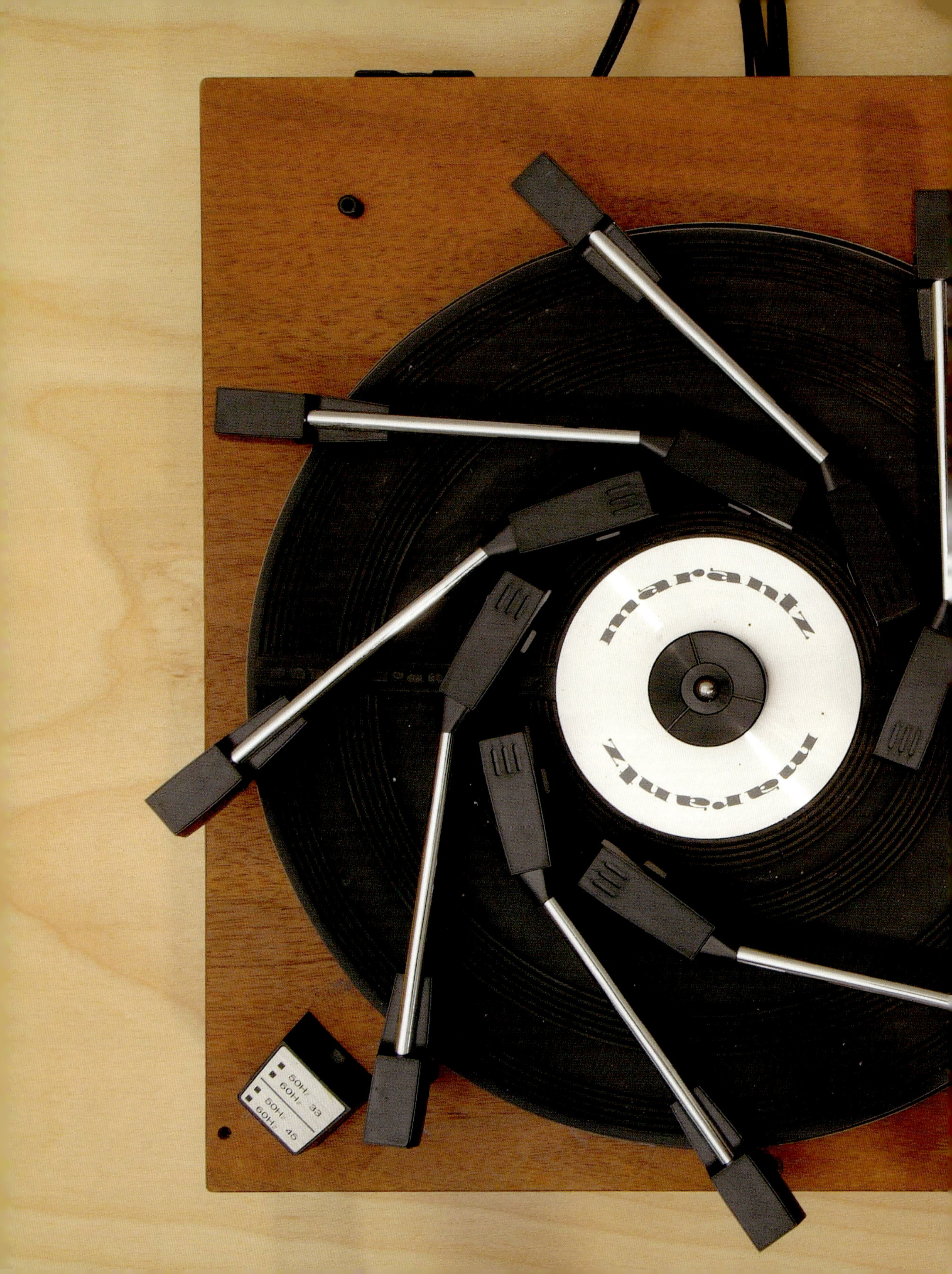
marantz
marantz

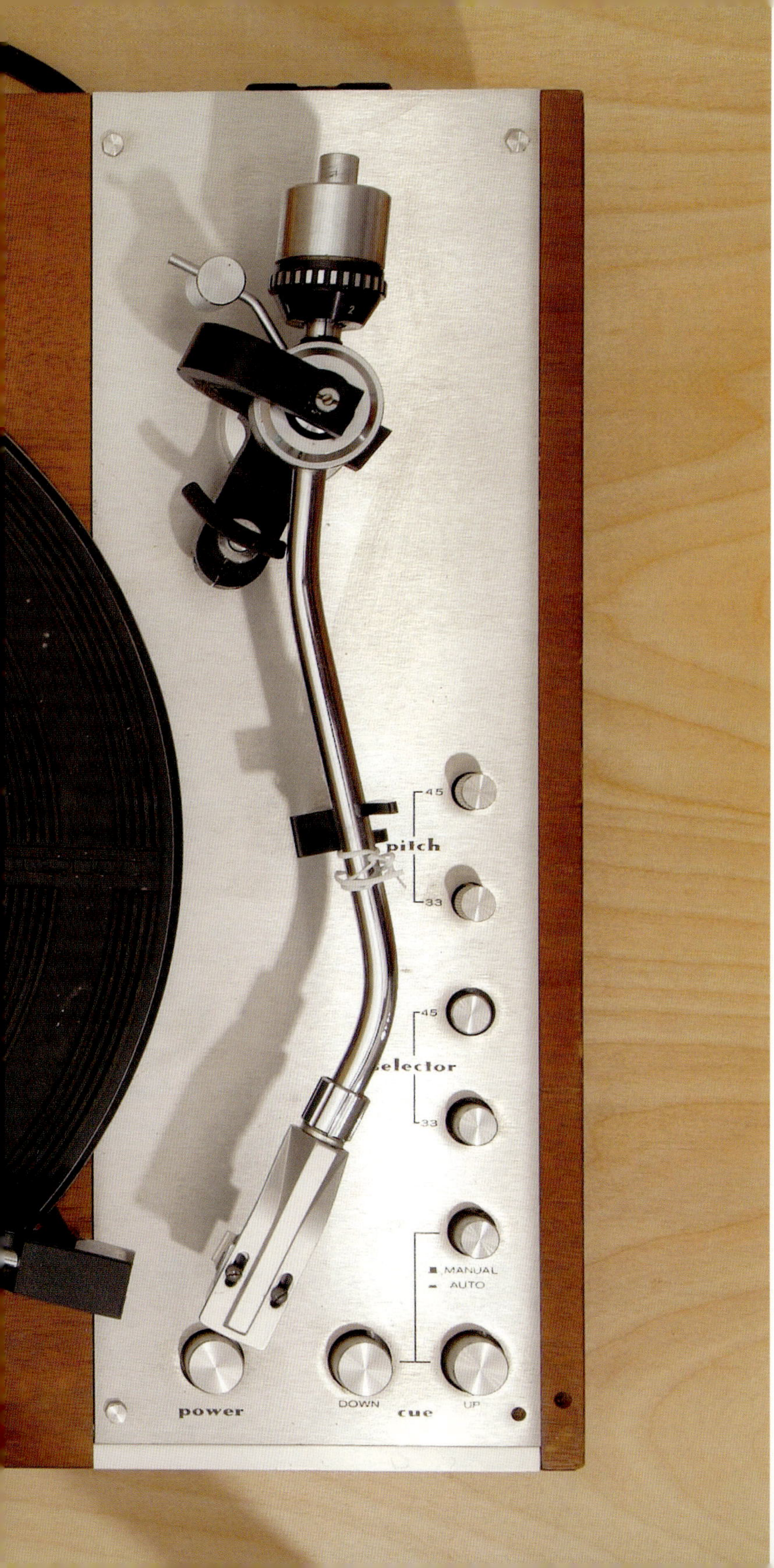
45
pitch
33
45
selector
33
MANUAL
AUTO
power
DOWN
cue
UP

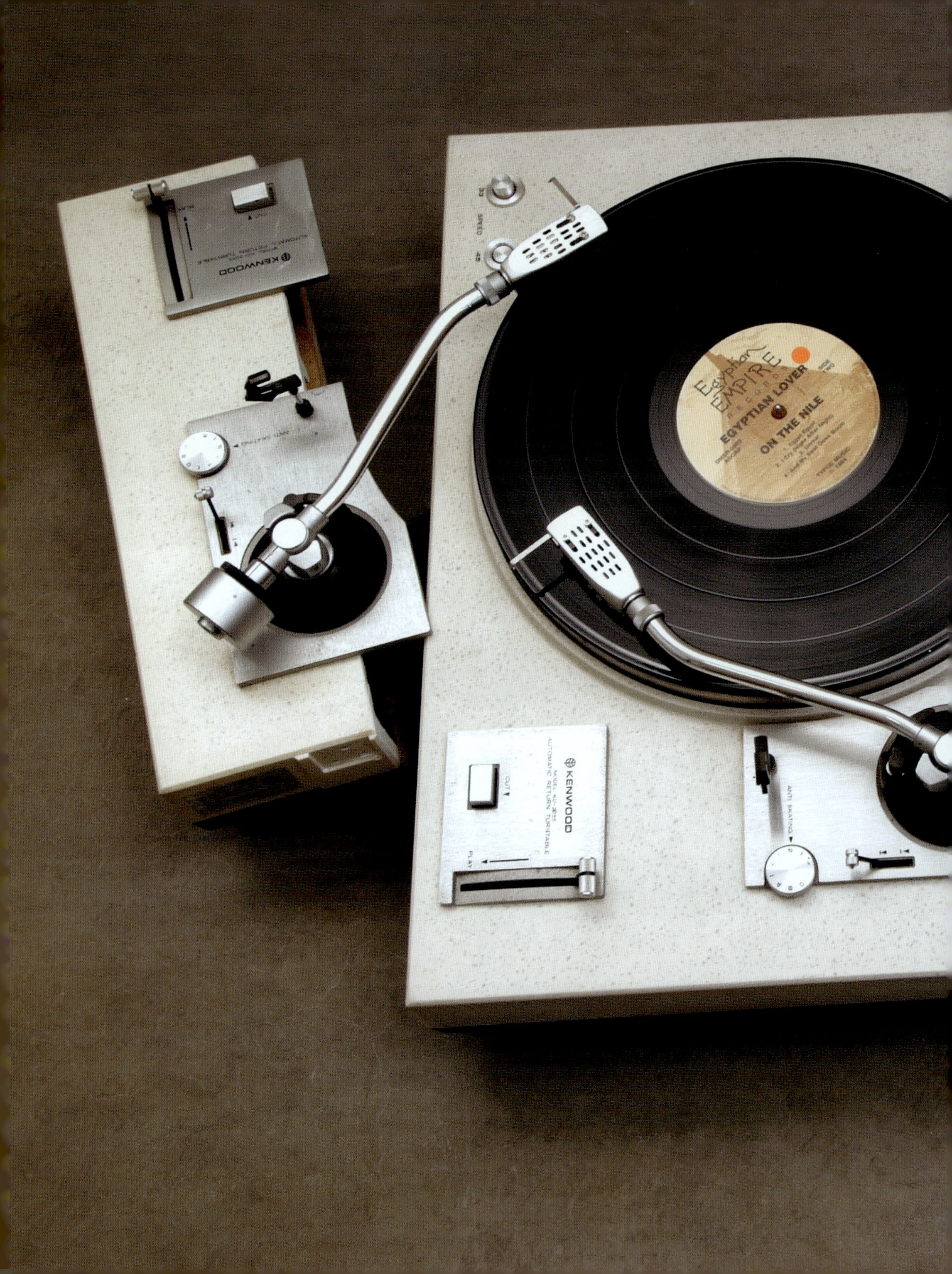

33
SPEED
45
Egyptian
EMPIRE
RECORDS
EGYPTIAN LOVER
ON THE NILE
KENWOOD
AUTOMATIC RETURN TURNTABLE
OUT
PLAY
ANTI SKATING

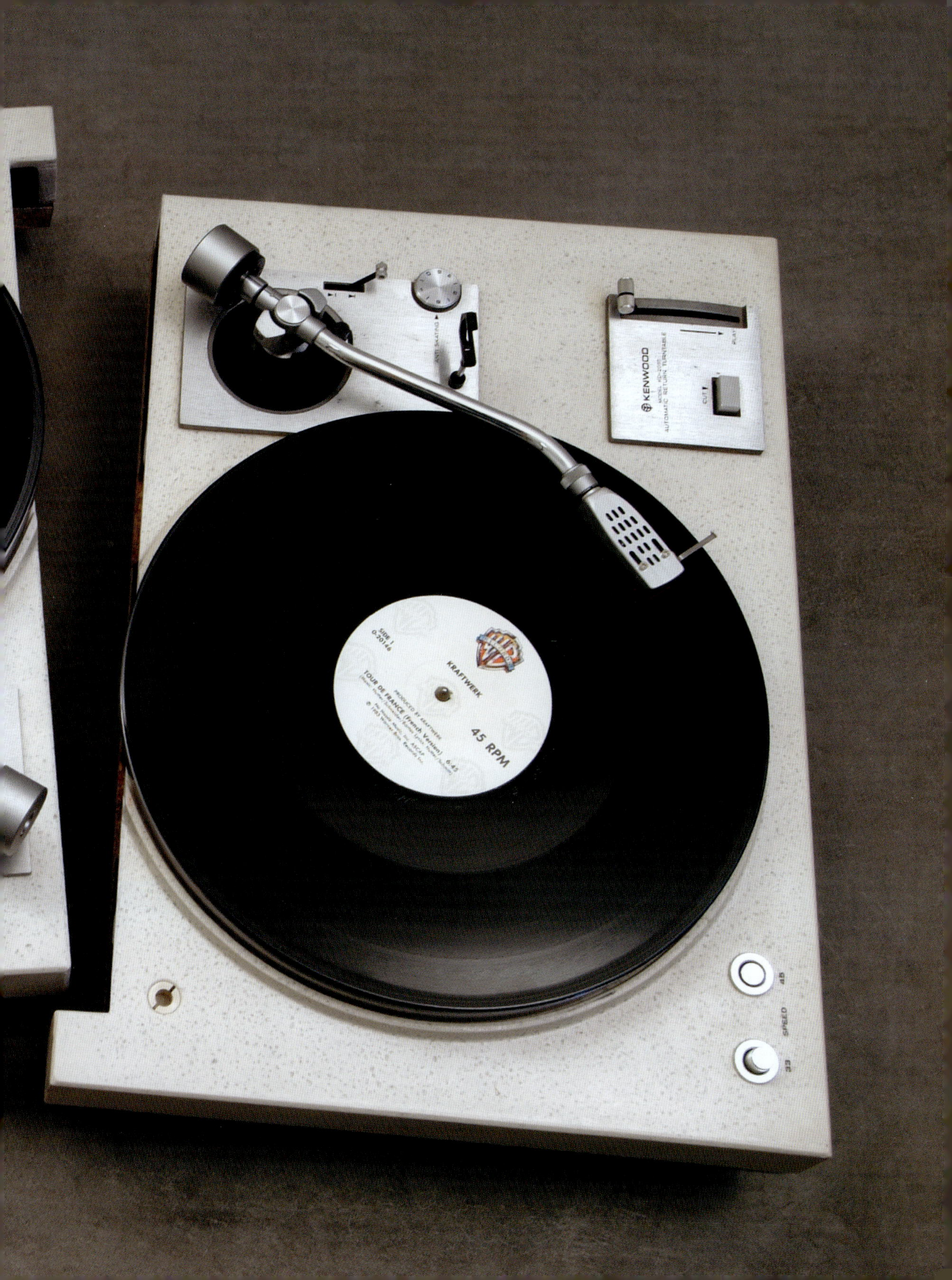
KENWOOD
AUTOMATIC RETURN TURNTABLE
PLAY
CUT
ANTI-SKATING
SIDE 1
0-20146
KRAFTWERK
PRODUCED BY KRAFTWERK
TOUR DE FRANCE (French Version) 6:45
45 RPM
SPEED
45
33

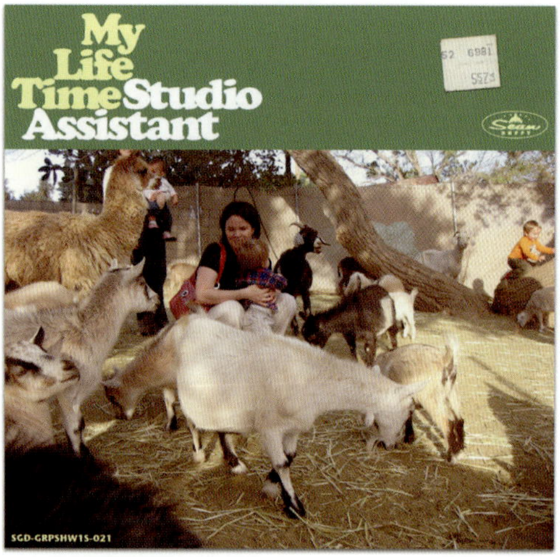
My Life Time Studio Assistant
SGD-GRPSHW15-021

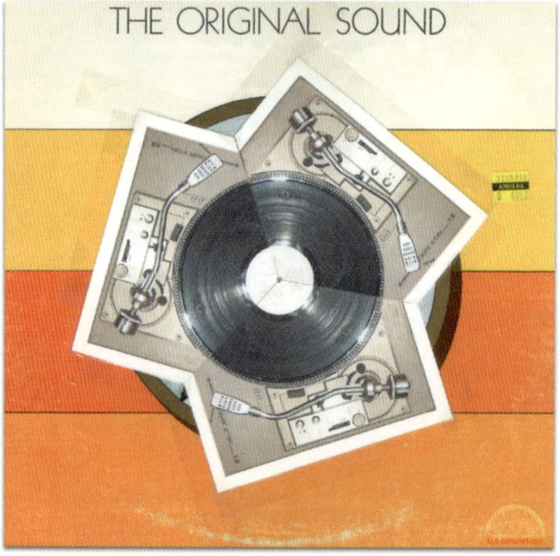
THE ORIGINAL SOUND

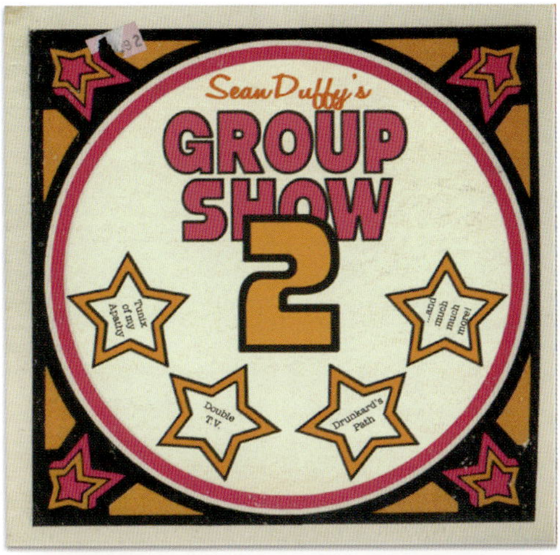
Sean Duffy's
GROUP
SHOW
2
Tunix of my Apathy
...and much much more!
Double T.V.
Drunkard's Path

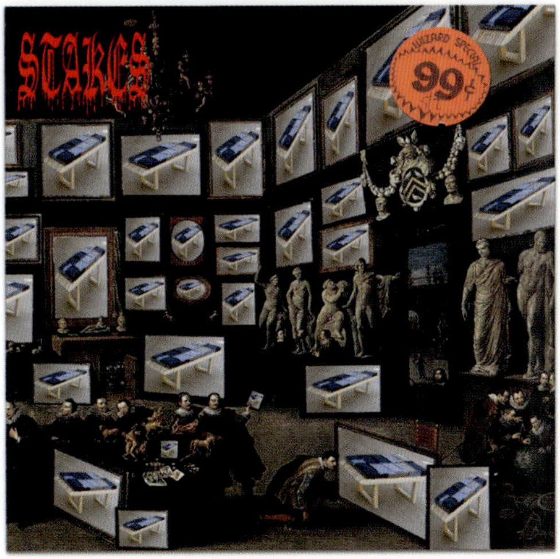
STAKES
WIZARD SPECIAL
99¢

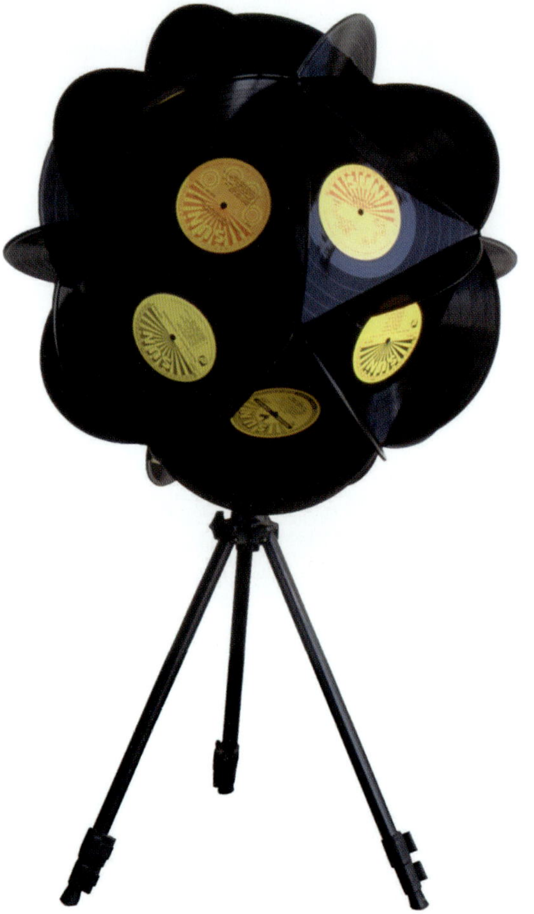

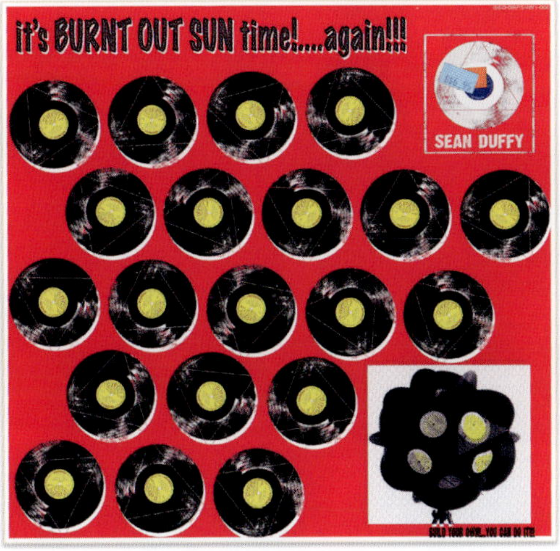
it's BURNT OUT SUN time!....again!!!
SEAN DUFFY

Sean
DUFFY
UNLIMITED EDITION

Q & *A*

with

VERONICA FERNANDEZ

At what time did music enter your life?

I started listening to music in junior high. I grew up in the hills of East County San Diego, where the radio reception was terrible and often overlapped with Mexican radio stations. I'd listen to it anyway, and I think this is where my interest in overlapping sound developed.

I didn't become a super fan of music until college. I started going to concerts, collecting records, and I deejayed at KSDT, my college radio station. That was when I fell hard for music and turntables. This was during the 80s, when there was a lot of noise and experimental sound. We had a great set-up where there were three turntables, with two right next to each other. You could swing the tonearm of one over onto the other and have two tonearms on one record. This is where I did the first experiments with the echo effect you hear in my turntable pieces. It's when you have two, three, even eight needles playing one song on a record and because they're in the same groove, they create an echo.

I view the breadth of your work as including many tempos playing at once. Do you consciously think of your work and artistic practice as it relates specifically to musical terminology? Terms that come to mind are *mash-up, sampling, loop tones.*

No, I don't, but I've heard people use *mash-up* in relation to my work and think that's kind of interesting. I don't think of myself as a musician but more as an instrument-maker. I make a device that creates a kind of accidental sound and set it up for somebody else to play.

My practice really comes from having a short attention span, which is difficult in an art career. I think that the art world values the long, deep conversation and in-depth focus. I remember sharing a studio with a painter who would do the classic thing of sitting in his chair, contemplating his work for hours on end. I just couldn't do that. I can concentrate for about 20 minutes—about the length of an LP side. So I developed a strategy for making work, which was to work on three or four things at once. If I was working on something and became distracted or bored, I could immediately stop—before I messed it up—and begin working on something else.

But the role of the accidental seems paramount in your work.

Yes, accidents are very important, and working on multiple things at once encourages them. Some of my biggest successes came from making an accident and then stepping away for an hour, a week or however long it took until I could figure out the next step. I think to myself, "This accident happened. Let's see what it means."

Let's talk about your interest in record albums and how you began incorporating them into your work.

I love the way record stores present information—how they're a database of sorts. Each album, with its cover art and information on the back, is a bit of data. They're organized into categories and bins. You have the valuable ones displayed on the wall, the cheap ones in bins on the floor, and, in the middle, the ones for browsing. I decided to sort out my work the same way.

In 2005, I started documenting my work as actual album covers where I would create an LP or 45 for each work, influence and idea. I filed them into categories like *this show, thoughts, family, old gold*, and so on. I liked being able to shuffle in that way. Books and art catalogs are designed to be read from start to finish. With records, you can easily change their order or the categories. They can go up on the wall or down in the dollar bin. I felt that was a nice way to look at my career.

In trying to reproduce the feel of records, I found

that they weren't always well-designed. They were often done quickly and sloppily. The 50s records had their off-register printing and the 70s records had their cheesy pictures. It was great but challenging to put something together that was "off" on purpose. I allowed myself the freedom to make an imperfect object, but it had to be flawed in just the "right" way in order to look like a record.

It's interesting to hear you talk about this fast and sloppy off-register technique to the album covers. Was your use of the screen-printing process born out of your love of albums, as opposed to referencing Andy Warhol and his screen-printing? I know that his work has been brought up in relation to yours before.

Warhol is certainly an influence, and I think that there is a relationship to his work, but not in my use of screen-printing. When I taught at UC Irvine, I used to ask my students, "What would Andy Warhol do today?" In your dorm room, you have more than Andy Warhol ever had. You have a computer, a scanner, a digital camera, Photoshop and a printer. You can crank stuff out all night. Warhol used screen-printing because, at the time, it was the best way he could make his work. But I don't know if he'd be screen-printing now.

My interest in screen-printing mainly came out of my love of old style album covers and T-shirts. I learned to screen-print in college just so that I could make my own shirts. It can be such a precise process, though I find if you do it too well, the end result looks bad. The more loose and messy you are, the better the screens look. If you can hold back from making everything precise, blend the colors, let things go off-register, they come out better.

The screen-printing process is just one way in which the theme of repetition comes up in your work.

Yes. Repetition and "the copy of the copy" are themes that have been occurring in my work for years. I like the idea of what it means to copy something. Or what it means to make the same gesture at a different time.

Lately, I have been getting a bit stuck on albums because they're a vernacular that isn't as familiar to the younger generation. Kids today just don't have the same relationship to them that I did in the 70s and 80s. Then again, half the records I bought for the last show were new pressings, so maybe it's not too archaic.

So with regard to albums becoming an antiquated part of our culture, your work, by virtue of the time in which it's being made, is part of our contemporary culture. But your concerns have to do with many things Americana, and with the past. How contemporary do you feel your work is? Is this even a concern of yours?

It's a big concern. I enjoy obsessing about where art is going, where it's been and what it should do. I do sometimes feel that I'm stuck in the past. Part of it started early on when I was doing work based on the original *Star Trek*. I thought maybe I should try to be "current" and work with new material, but new material didn't carry the same weight. *Star Trek* had become universal, even people who had never seen the show recognized it in my work. With art history, I'm never really sure where people are in time. Think of Ed Ruscha's painting, *Annie* (1965). [The comic strip Little Orphan] Annie was 40 years old at the time. Was he referencing the deep past? I don't think so. Or Andy Warhol's Coke bottle paintings...

I don't worry about this as much these days because I feel that using these types of icons that travel through time make sense. I've tried to be more contemporary, but contemporary culture draws so much from the past, it's difficult to figure out where to start.

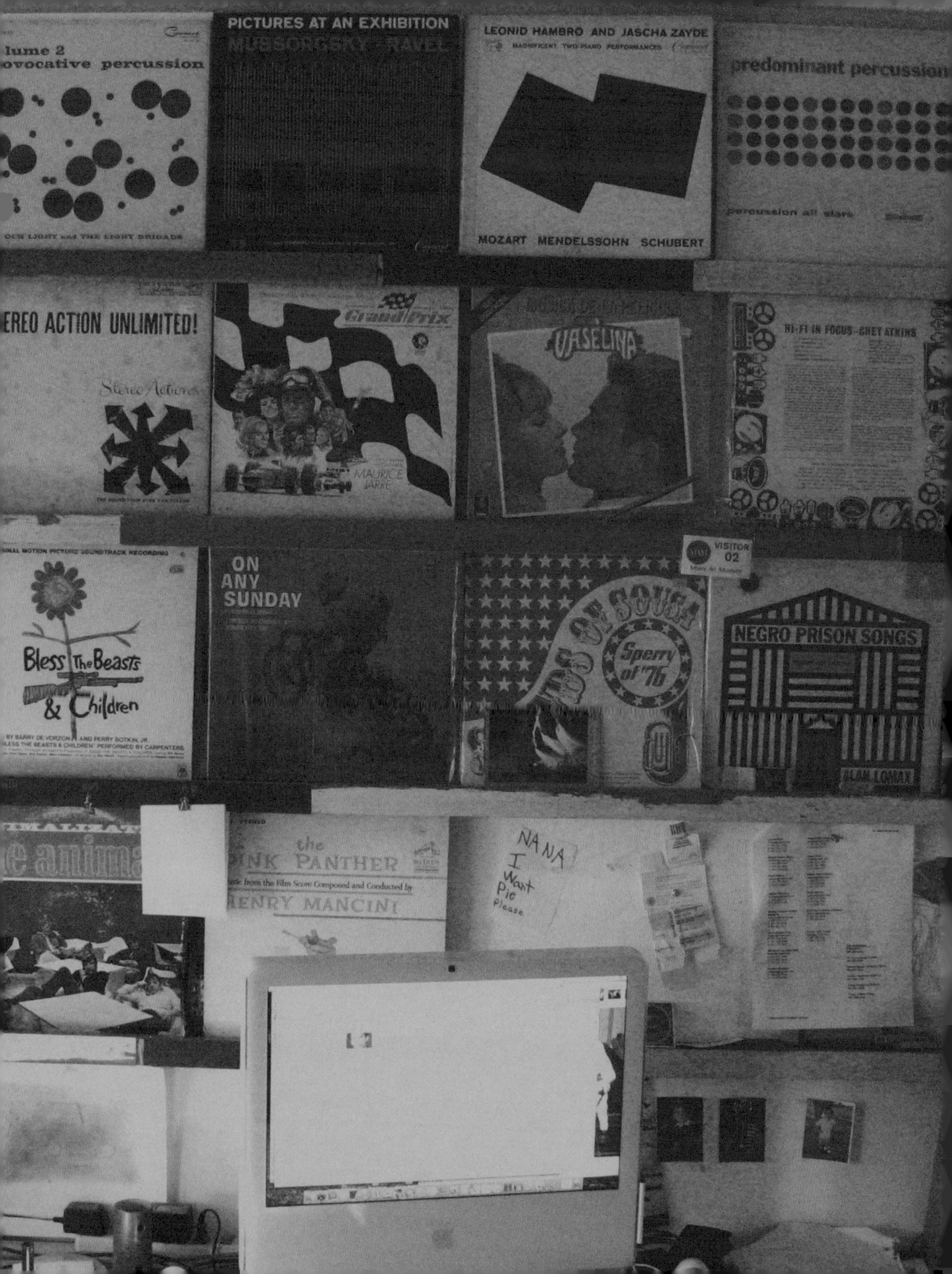

lume 2
ovocative percussion
PICTURES AT AN EXHIBITION
LEONID HAMBRO AND JASCHA ZAYDE
MOZART MENDELSSOHN SCHUBERT
predominant percussion
percussion all stars
EREO ACTION UNLIMITED!
Stereo Action
Grand Prix
MAURICE JARRE
VASELINA
HI-FI IN FOCUS—CHET ATKINS
Bless The Beasts & Children
ON ANY SUNDAY
VISITOR 02
Sperry of '76
NEGRO PRISON SONGS
ALAN LOMAX
the PINK PANTHER
HENRY MANCINI
NANA I Want Pie please

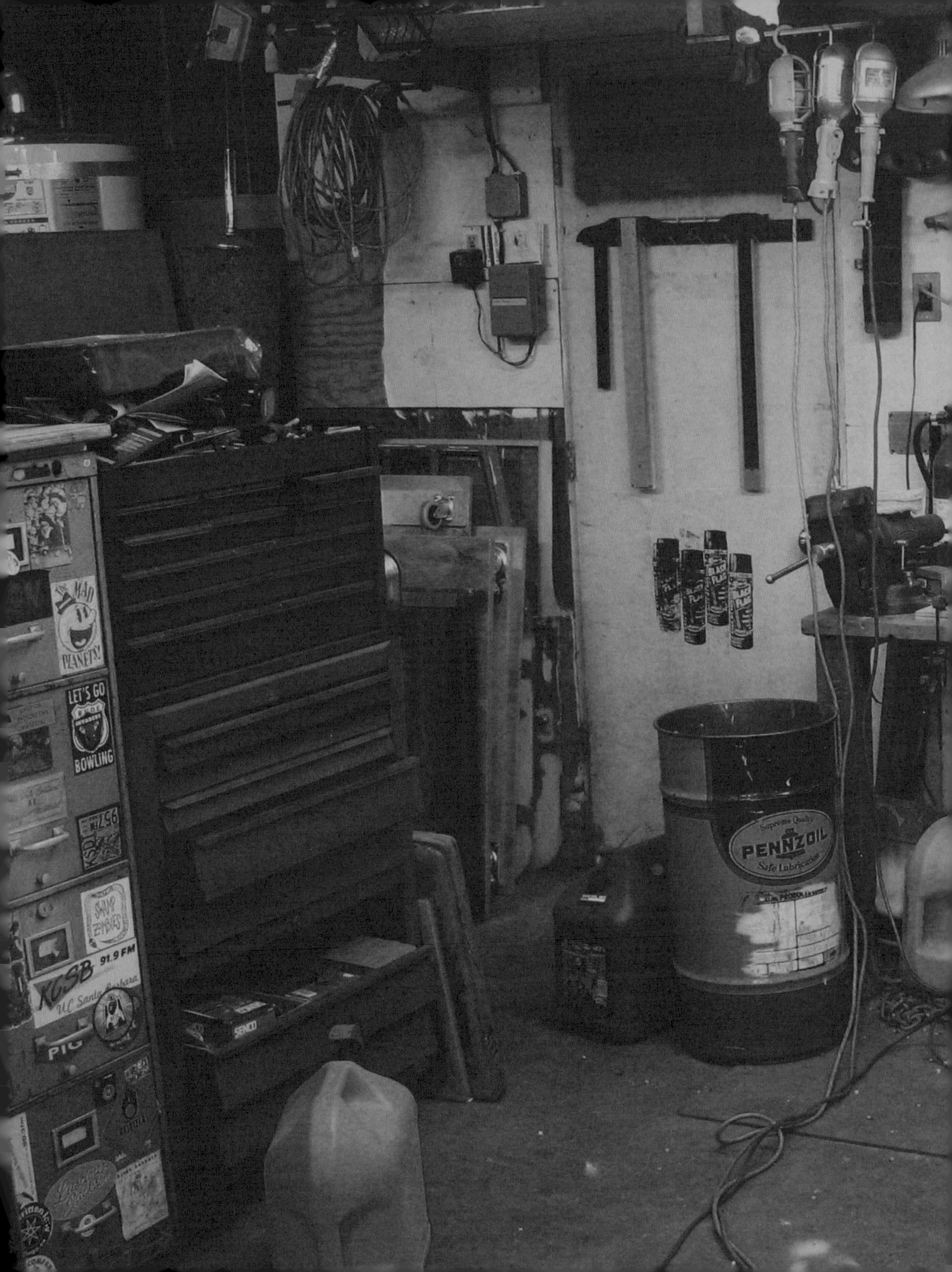
PLANETS!
LET'S GO
BOWLING
KCSB 91.9 FM
U.C. Santa Barbara
SENCO
Supreme Quality
PENNZOIL
Safe Lubrication

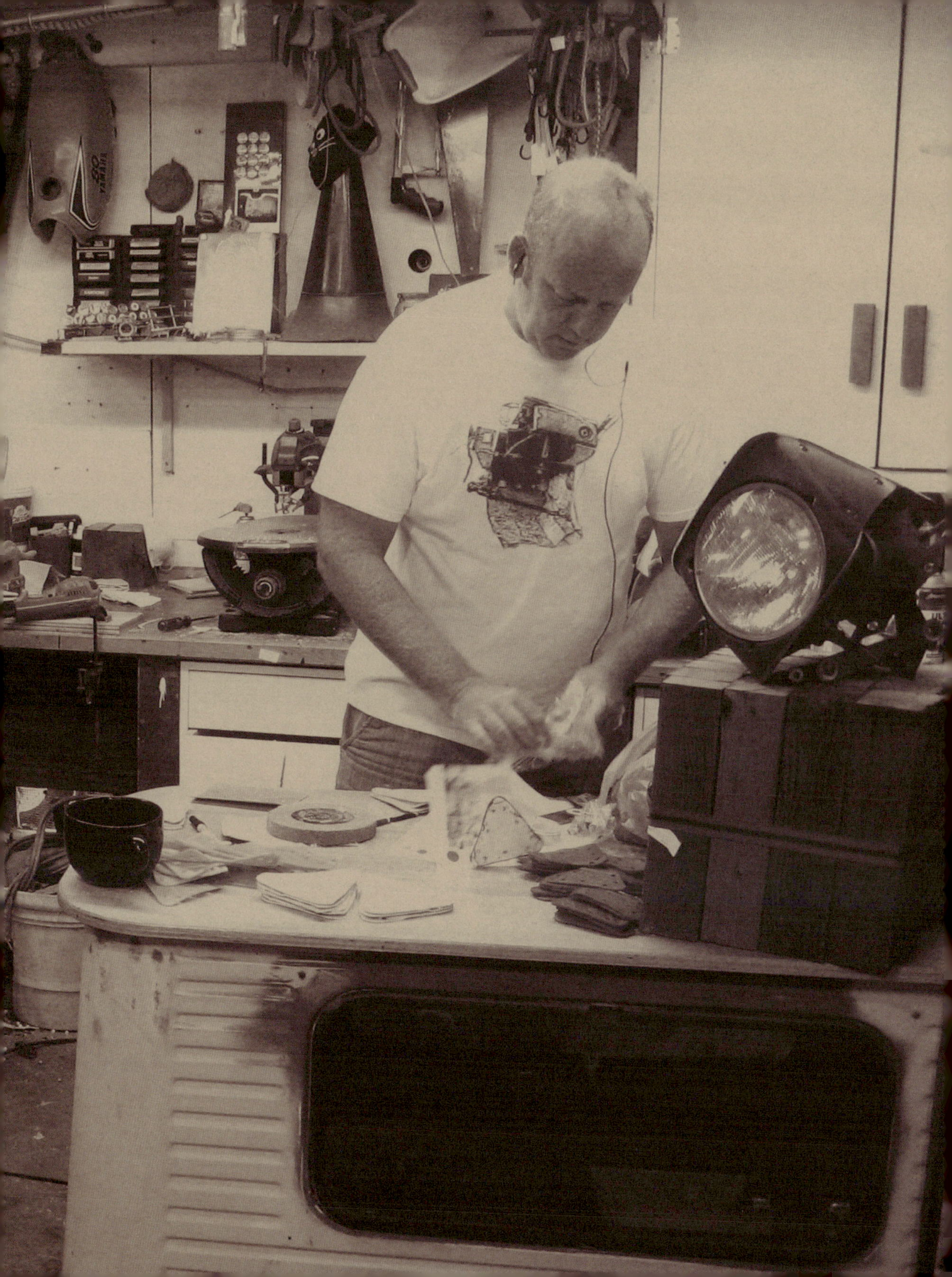

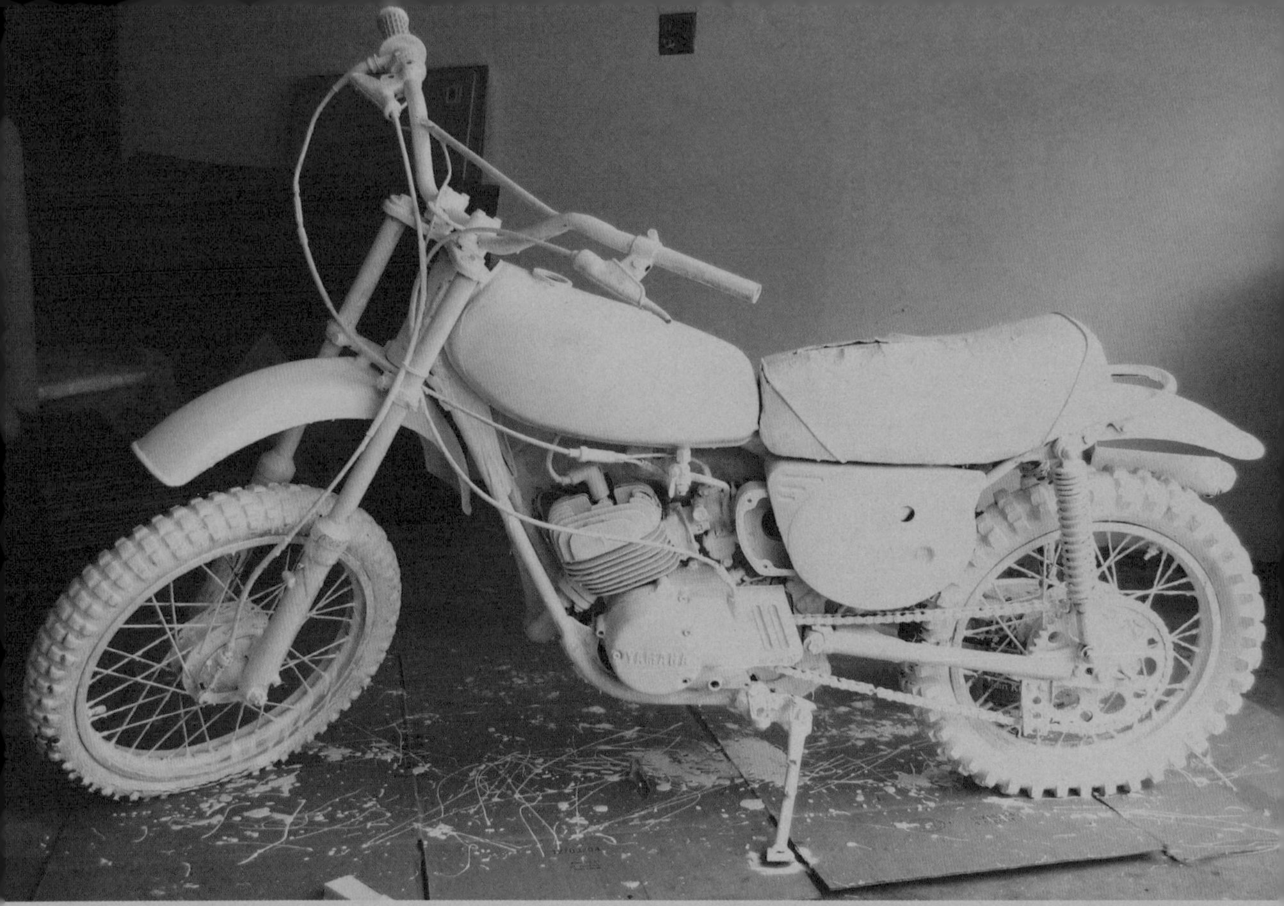
YAMAHA

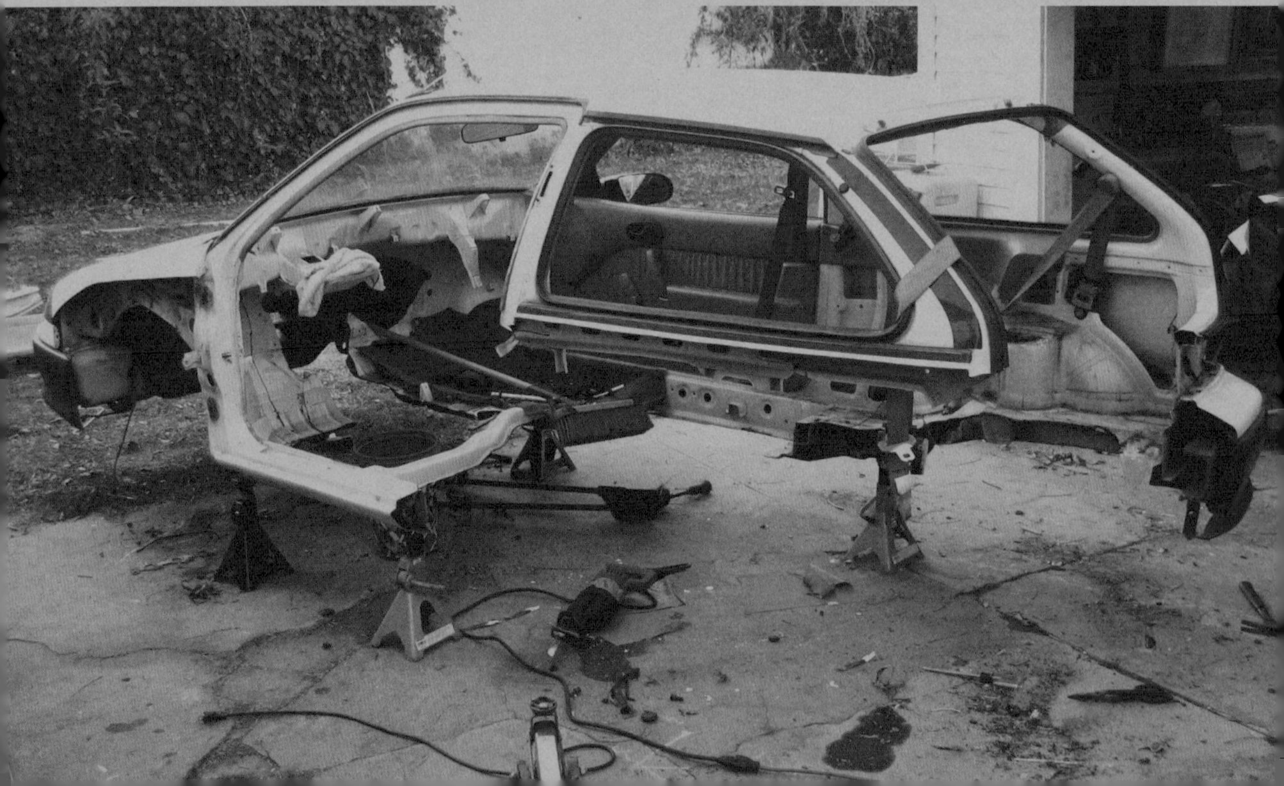

Let's talk about the idea of democracy. There is very much a democratic appeal to your work.

Democracy is an interesting word for it. I feel it's important to make work that's accessible on many levels so that anyone can engage with it. I want to see an adult appreciate a piece and have a kid fall in love with the same piece for a completely different reason. Art needs a "hook," but over time, it has to unfold into more complex ideas.

What do you wish to get across to your viewers by constantly referencing the familiar? Why is nostalgia so important to you?

The familiar is the access point in my work. We don't often notice how amazing the world we're in is. Using the familiar is my way of saying, "Step back, and look at what's going on around you."

Regarding nostalgia, I like telling stories, but can't write and don't want to make movies. I don't have that kind of temperament, so I try to tell stories that unfold in a way that allow people to inject their own ideas to create a larger narrative. I might not be able to put a story into words exactly, but I know how to make objects about it.

A lot of what I want to talk about is in the past—it's like Martin Scorsese or Sergio Leone films where they use different eras to address contemporary issues. I try to do the same within my art practice.

Let's discuss your use of "the machine."

When I started working with turntables, I came to love them as social machines. You turn on audio equipment when people come over. You turn off the TV; you should turn off your computer; but you always play music. Audio equipment is front and center for entertaining. To me, the design of the turntable makes a "look at this" statement.

Cars play a similar role; they're how we identify ourselves. They were harder for me to get into because they're loaded symbols. I struggle with the romantic notions we attach to cars because they're so exaggerated.

I also have problems with the idea of restoring cars and engines. In the process, we erase their histories. *Third Motorcycle* started with my old Yamaha YZ80, the third motorcycle I had growing up as a kid. My first thought was, "Oh, I'll fix it up for my kids." But I would have erased its history. All the dents, tears, stickers and rust would have been removed, and I would have eradicated my whole experience with this bike. Painting it preserved that experience.

So would the final object be something you consider authentic? How does the role of authenticity play into the work if you are reworking the original object?

I think it ends up being a documentation of the object with the object—a kind of thorough examination of it. The object is simultaneously authentic and a copy. I could have shown the old motorcycle, but people wouldn't really have looked at it the same way I would have. By copying it onto itself, I tried to convey how I saw that motorcycle as well as my experience with it. Some people were bothered that I used the actual bike for the painting. For me, it made perfect sense. If I had made a copy of the motorcycle, people would have been bogged down with "how did he do that?" By using the real one, it became more about "why did he do that?" which helped its story to unfold.

What would you say are some of your most successful works to date, and why?

That's a really tough question. I cycle through works I love so quickly. I'll find an old piece that I've completely forgotten about and say, "That's amazing! Why aren't I doing that now?" Then forget about it in two weeks. There are a couple pieces that really changed things for me though.

The first turntable, *Triple Turntable* in 2001, was a wonderful experience. I hadn't realized it would work as well as it did. People didn't immediately see it as an art object. They'd walk up to it and see it as a turntable, and then after a second, they'd see it was actually three turntables. That moment of confusion drew them in, and then they wanted to know everything about it.

The Grove had an immense scale and did almost everything right. The budget for the project was small, so I made everything roughly and cheaply. The tables were made out of property markers, and the turntables were really inexpensive. Because of its roughness, people immediately knew that they could interact with it, touch it, play the records. It was one of the first times I was able to get the audience to participate and respond in that way.

Also, *The Palette*, which was all about my new frugality of trying to use the stuff that was sitting around the studio. It showed how listening to music was just as integral to my art practice as the actual work.

There is this great quote by artist Ryan McGinley, who became known several years ago after taking this heartfelt series of photographs of fans who attended Morrissey concerts. He said, "These are my songs, just like they are everyone else's, but they are still mine." Do you feel a connection to this?

Yes. I couldn't tell my life story without some of these albums, like The Beach Boys' *Pet Sounds* or The Clash's *London Calling*. I'm trying to tell a story about how I see things along with what I see, and I just have to refer to sound. I'm not painting pictures of cornfields or haystacks because that's not what's outside my door every morning. Every morning, I'm listening to the radio, driving in the car, watching TV.

I feel like you need to live a lot as an artist in order to be able to make work. Too often I see artists whose whole world is art, and they can only make work that's about art because they're so wrapped up in it. You've got to have an existence outside of your practice—that's whats going to inform the work. If you are trying to talk about the contemporary world, you have to talk about the stuff that bombards you constantly. And I think that most of that stuff is great.

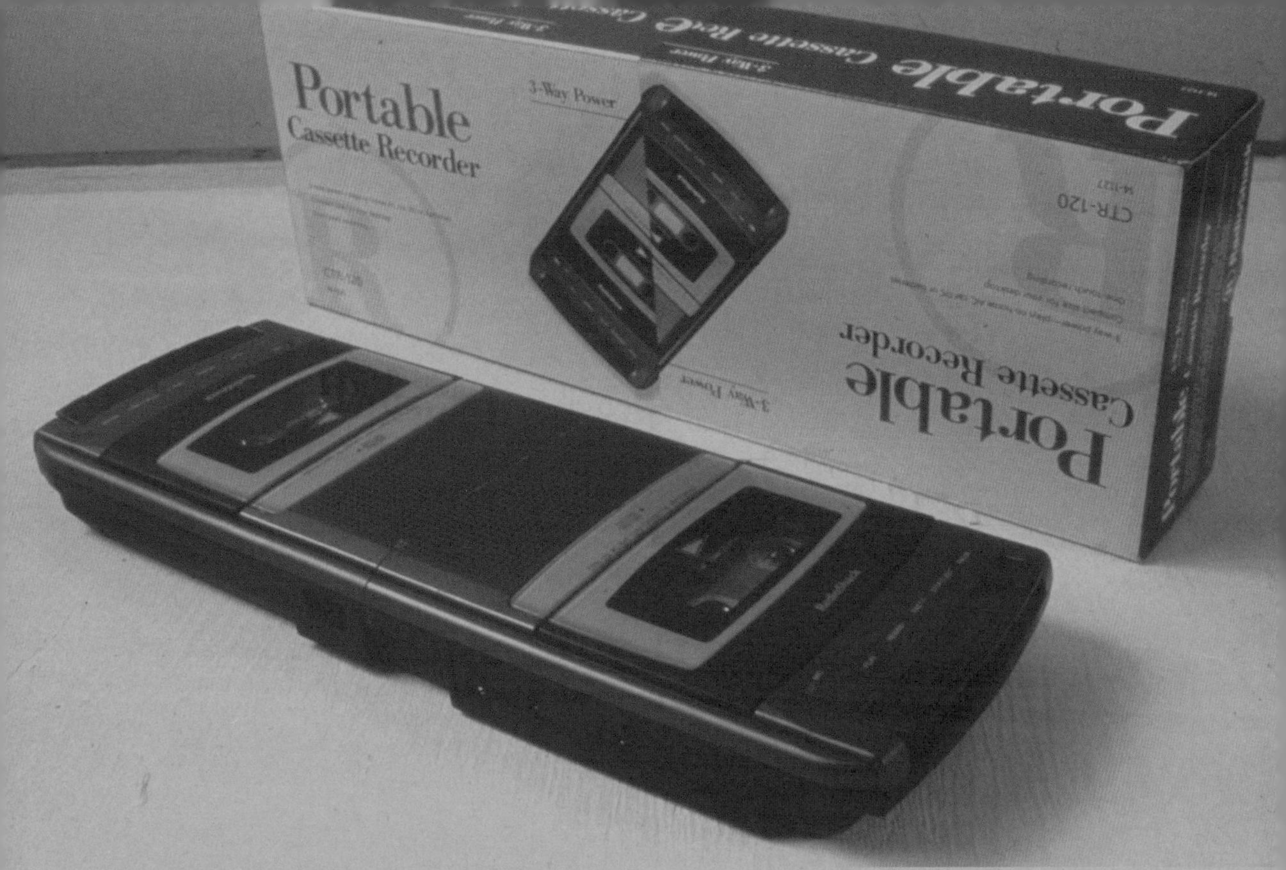
Portable
Cassette Recorder
3-Way Power
CTR-120
Portable
Cassette Recorder

A

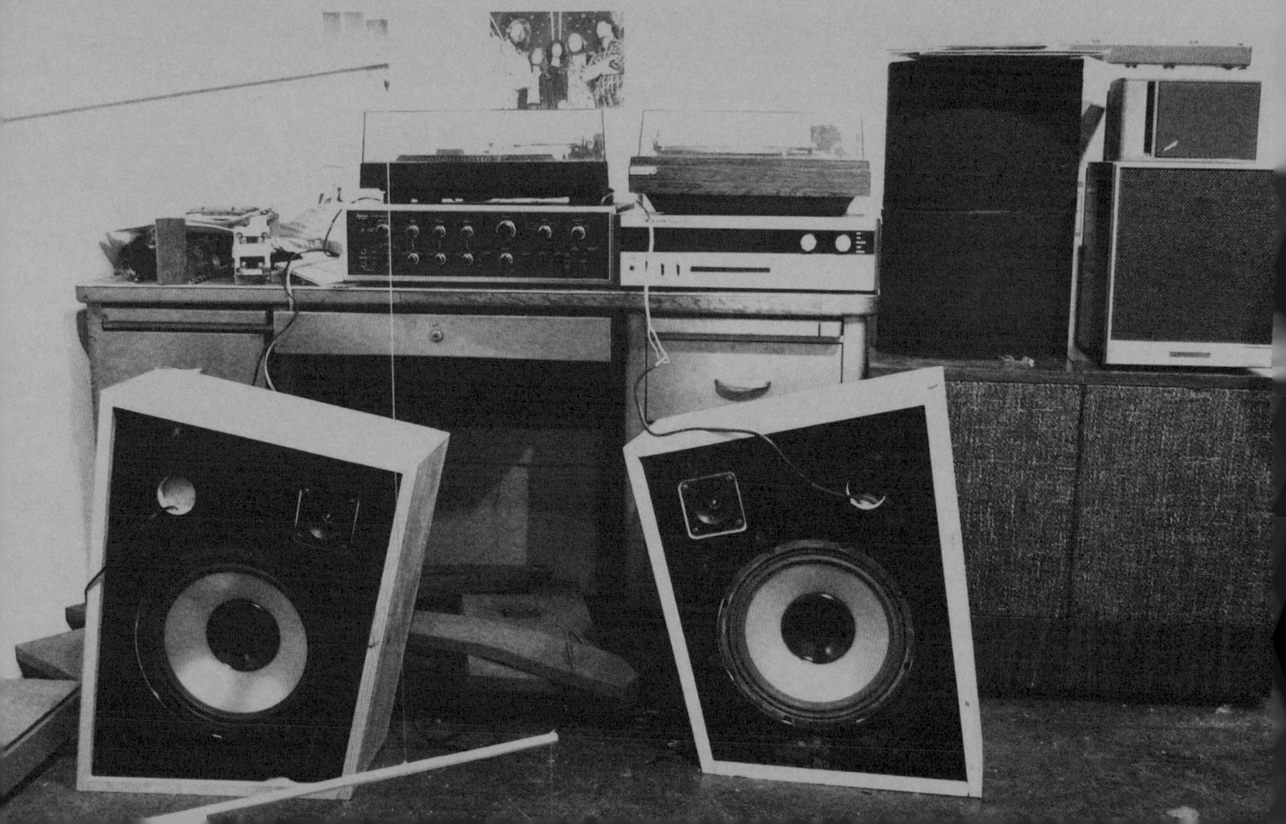

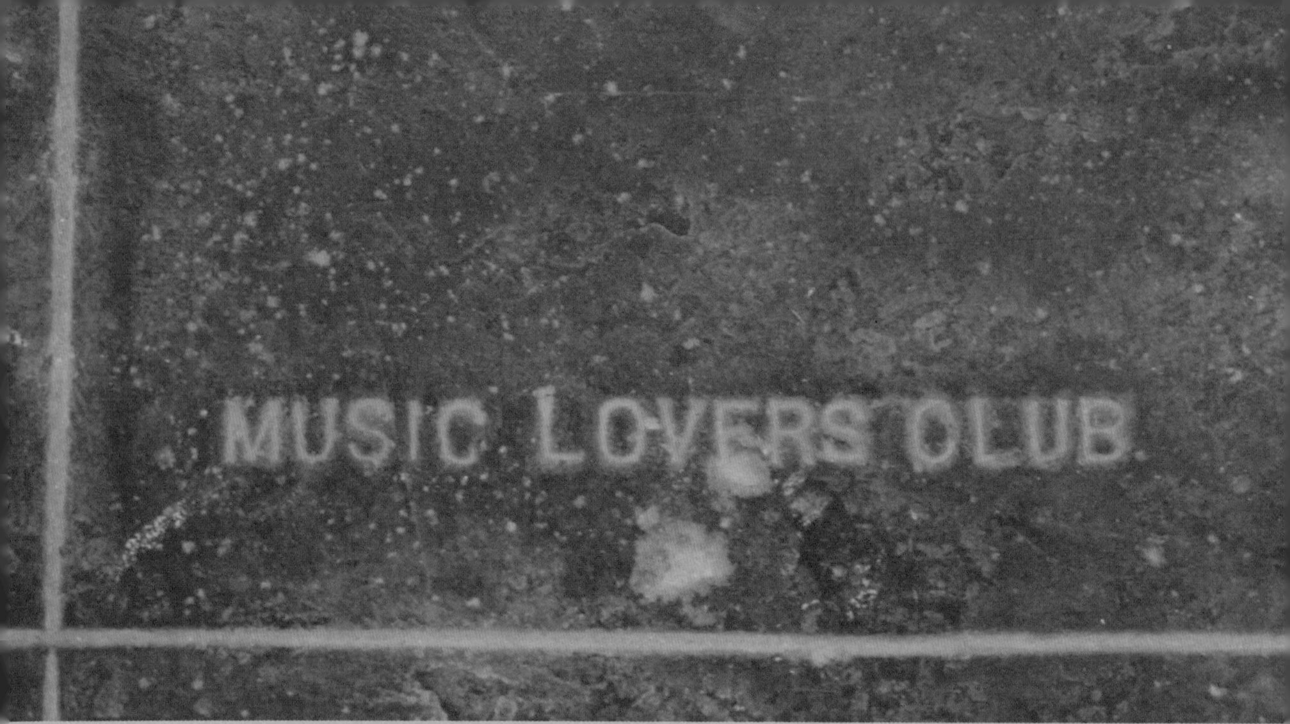
MUSIC LOVERS CLUB

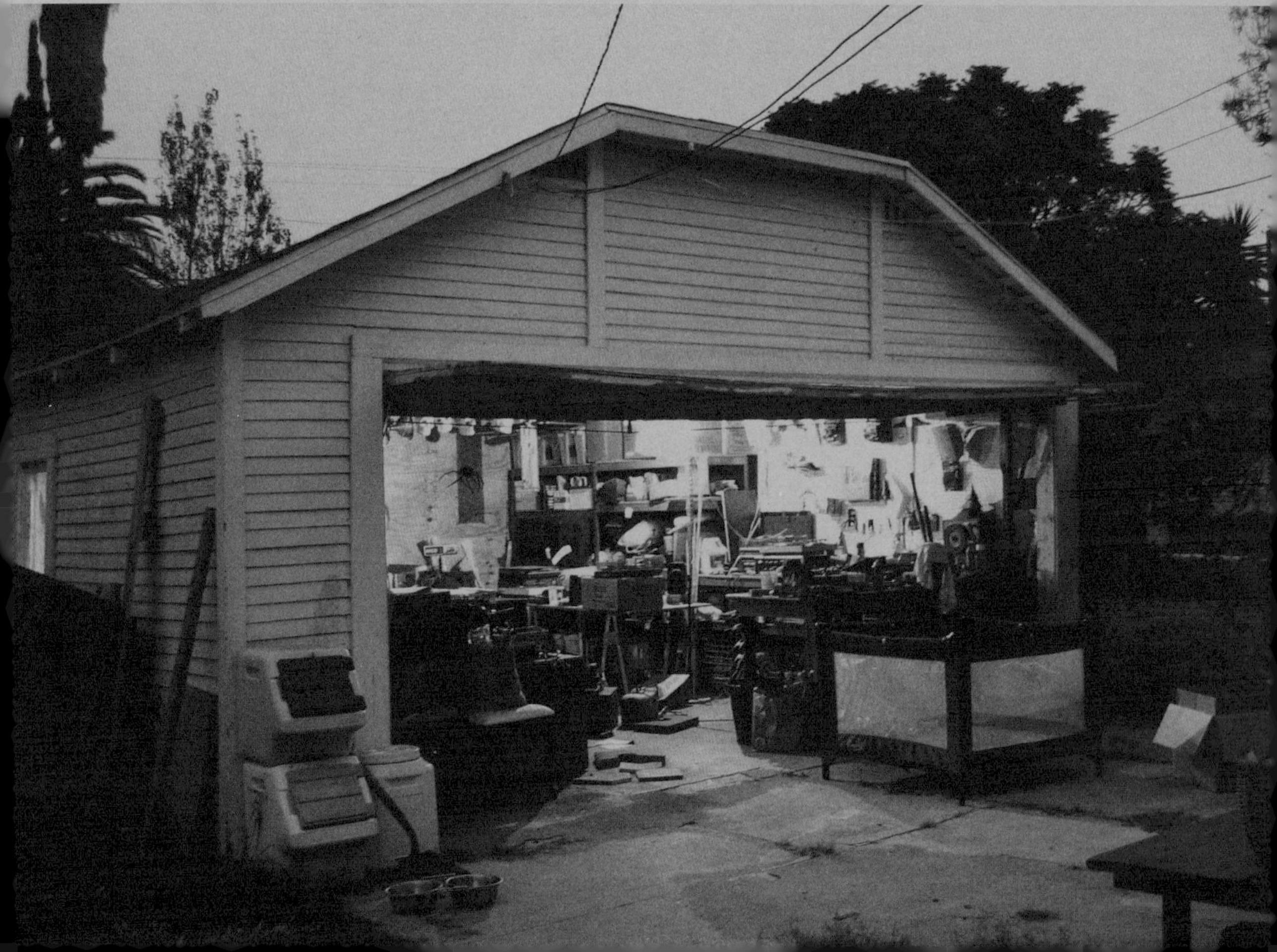

VERONICA FERNANDEZ is an art consultant and principal of FINE ART ADVISING SERVICES, an advisory that builds comprehensive contemporary art collections for private individuals around the United States. While Ms. Fernandez specializes in placing artworks made within the last five decades, her dedication and focus is on emerging and mid-career artists based in Los Angeles, a city where she believes some of the most challenging and compelling work is currently produced.

She is happy to have stumbled upon Mr. Duffy in her backyard.

WWW.FINEARTADVISING.COM

CATALOG

Cover

Group Show
2006
wood shelf, archival inkjet prints in clear plastic sleeves
92" x 41" x 10"
Courtesy of SUSANNE VIELMETTER LOS ANGELES PROJECTS / Photo Credit: GENE OGAMI

Plates

01 *Individual Record: "Tunix of My Apathy"*
2007
archival inkjet print in clear plastic sleeve
12" x 12"
Courtesy of the artist

02 *Individual Record: "Group Show"*
2006
archival inkjet print in clear plastic sleeve
12" x 12"
Courtesy of the artist

03 *Individual Record: "Hand to Mouth"*
2006
archival inkjet print in clear plastic sleeve
12" x 12"
Courtesy of the artist

04 *Individual Record: "Temporary Worker"*
2006
archival inkjet print in clear plastic sleeve
12" x 12"
Courtesy of the artist

05 *Individual Record: "Generic Back"*
2006
archival inkjet print in clear plastic sleeve
12" x 12"
Courtesy of the artist

06 *Individual Record: "Ms. Hurst Shifter"*
2006
archival inkjet print in clear plastic sleeve
12" x 12"
Courtesy of the artist

07 Study for *Jazz & Smoke*
2003
two modified Garrard 6/300 turntables
33" x 19" x 8"
Courtesy of the artist

08 *Body & Soul*
2002
two turntables, wood, Formica, two speakers, three records (Thelonious Monk, Charles Mingus, Rahsaan Roland Kirk)
22" x 16" x 8.5"
Courtesy of SUSANNE VIELMETTER LOS ANGELES PROJECTS / Collection of DENNIS AND DEBRA SCHOLL, MIAMI BEACH, FL / Photo Credit: GENE OGAMI

09 *Individual Record: "Television"*
2007
archival inkjet print in clear plastic sleeve
7" x 7"
Courtesy of the artist

10 *Individual Record: "Jazz and Smoke"*
2011
archival inkjet print in clear plastic sleeve
12" x 12"
Courtesy of the artist

11 *Triple-turntable*
2001
three Yamaha YP-B2 turntables, mixer, amp, speakers, canvas, stretcher bars
40" x 24" x 24"
Courtesy of SUSANNE VIELMETTER LOS ANGELES PROJECTS / Collection of MIKE MEHRING, NEW YORK, NY

12 Study for *Double Television*
2007
two flat screen TVs, DVD players, DVDs, wood, LPs
18" x 38" x 46"
Courtesy of the artist

13 *Too late to save your heart*
2003
three album covers, permanent marker
12.5" x 12.75" each

Courtesy of Susanne Vielmetter Los Angeles Projects / Photo Credit: Gene Ogami

14 *It's never too late*
2003
album cover, Sharpie marker
25" x 12.5"
Courtesy of Susanne Vielmetter Los Angeles Projects / Photo Credit: Gene Ogami

15 *I'm the singer, you're the song*
2003
album cover, Sharpie marker
25" x 12.5"
Courtesy of Susanne Vielmetter Los Angeles Projects / Collection of Wilhelm Schuerman, Aachen, Germany / Photo Credit: Gene Ogami

16 *Tonight you belong to me*
2003
album cover, Sharpie marker
25" x 12.5"
Courtesy of Susanne Vielmetter Los Angeles Projects / Photo Credit: Gene Ogami

17 *Touch of Madness*
2003
nine LPs, permanent marker
40" x 40" overall
Courtesy of Susanne Vielmetter Los Angeles Projects / Photo Credit: Gene Ogami

18 *The Good, The Bad, and The Ugly*
2006
two Rek-o-Kut turntables, wood, aluminum, hardware, mixer, amplifier, speakers, Ennio Morricone LPs
9" x 26" x 23" turntable, 18" x 30" x 30" pedestal
Courtesy of Susanne Vielmetter Los Angeles Projects / Collection of Greg Feldman, New York, NY / Photo Credit: Gene Ogami

19 *Individual Record: "Triple Victrola"*
2009
archival inkjet print in clear plastic sleeve
10" x 10"
Courtesy of the artist

20 *Triple Victrola*
2003
three reproduction victrolas, desk, paint
59" x 31" x 31"
Courtesy of Susanne Vielmetter Los Angeles Projects / Collection of Michael and Sirje Gold, Los Angeles, CA /Photo Credit: Gene Ogami

21 *Triple Victrola* (Detail view)
2003
three reproduction victrolas, desk, paint
59" x 31" x 31"
Courtesy of Susanne Vielmetter Los Angeles Projects / Collection of Michael and Sirje Gold, Los Angeles, CA /Photo Credit: Gene Ogami

22 *The Good, The Bad, and The Ugly II*
2006
three original album records, one unique album cover
12" x 38.5", 12" x 12" each
Courtesy of Susanne Vielmetter Los Angeles Projects / Photo Credit: Gene Ogami

23 *Individual Record: "Waiting"*
2007
archival inkjet print in clear plastic sleeve
7" x 7"
Courtesy of the artist

24 *Individual Record: "The Grove Again"*
2007
archival inkjet print in clear plastic sleeve
12" x 12"
Courtesy of the artist

25 *The Grove*
2006–2007
installation of 18 turntables, over 200 speakers at Luckman Gallery, California State university, Los Angeles, CA, January 13–March 3, 2007
Courtesy of the Luckman Gallery, Los Angeles, CA

26 *Temporary Worker* (Installation view)
Susanne Vielmetter Los Angeles Projects, October 16–November 13, 2004
Courtesy of Susanne Vielmetter Los Angeles Projects / Photo Credit: Gene Ogami

27 *Fortress*
2004
file cabinets, redwood
80" x 30" x 20"
Courtesy of Susanne Vielmetter Los Angeles Projects / Collection of The Nora Eccles Harrison Museum, University of Utah / Photo Credit: Gene Ogami

28 *Waiting #3*
2004
office chair, plants, soil
33" x 120" x 24"
Courtesy of Susanne Vielmetter Los Angeles Projects / Photo Credit: Gene Ogami

29 *Steelcase*
2004
file cabinets, redwood
52" x 15" x 56"
Courtesy of Susanne Vielmetter Los Angeles Projects / Photo Credit: Gene Ogami

30 *Can't Stop It* (Installation view)
Susanne Vielmetter Los Angeles Projects, November 7–December 19, 2009
Courtesy of Susanne Vielmetter Los Angeles Projects / Photo Credit: Robert Wedemeyer

31 *I Can't Complain*
2009
wood plank, found jars, collected materials
72" x 6" x 15"
Courtesy of Susanne Vielmetter Los Angeles Projects / Photo Credit: Robert Wedemeyer

32 *Doors*
2009
two car doors with fluorescent light fixtures
47" x 39" x 16" each
Courtesy of Susanne Vielmetter Los Angeles Projects / Photo Credit: Robert Wedemeyer

33 *Small Block*
2009
oil paint on Chevy small block engine, with engine stand
40 x 30" x 47"
Courtesy of Susanne Vielmetter Los Angeles Projects / Photo Credit: Robert Wedemeyer

34 *Can't Stop It* (Installation view)
Susanne Vielmetter Los Angeles Projects, November 7–December 19, 2009
Courtesy of Susanne Vielmetter Los Angeles Projects / Photo Credit: Robert Wedemeyer

35 *Los Angeles* (Detail view)
2009
acrylic on scrap wood
104" x 401" x 2"
(256 album covers, 12" x 12" each on eight shelves)
Courtesy of Susanne Vielmetter Los Angeles Projects / Photo Credit: Robert Wedemeyer

36 *Dropping Gold*
2010
cut Art Forum magazine (Summer 2009), cut Art in America magazine (October 2009)
20" x 15"
Courtesy of Susanne Vielmetter Los Angeles Projects / Photo Credit: Robert Wedemeyer

37 *Art News April 1998, Art Forum May 2009, Modern Painters September 2007*
2009
cut Art Forum magazine, cut Modern Painters magazine, cut Art News magazine
16.5" x 22" x 16"
Courtesy of Susanne Vielmetter Los Angeles Projects / Photo Credit: Robert Wedemeyer

38 *Can't Stop It* (Installation view)
Susanne Vielmetter Los Angeles Projects, November 7–December 19, 2009
Courtesy of Susanne Vielmetter Los Angeles Projects / Photo Credit: Robert Wedemeyer

39 *Art Forum December 2009*
2010
cut Art Forum magazine
10.5" x 10.5" x 0.5"
Courtesy of Susanne Vielmetter Los Angeles Projects / Photo Credit: Robert Wedemeyer

40 *Art Forum January 2009*
2009
cut Art Forum magazine
10.5" x 10.5" x 0.5"
Courtesy of Susanne Vielmetter Los Angeles Projects / Photo Credit: Robert Wedemeyer

41 *Art Forum February 2009*
2009
cut Art Forum magazine
10.5" x 10.5" x 0.5"
Courtesy of Susanne Vielmetter Los Angeles Projects / Photo Credit: Robert Wedemeyer

42 *Art Forum Summer 2008*
2009
cut Art Forum magazine
10.5" x 10.5" x 0.5"
Courtesy of Susanne Vielmetter Los Angeles Projects / Photo Credit: Robert Wedemeyer

43 *Individual Record: "BOG"*
2006
archival inkjet print in clear plastic sleeve
12" x 12"
Courtesy of the artist

44 *Individual Record: "First Helmet"*
2006
archival inkjet print in clear plastic sleeve
12" x 12"
Courtesy of the artist

45 *Third Motorcycle*
2006
oil on motorcycle
38" x 62" x 30"
Courtesy of Susanne Vielmetter Los Angeles Projects / Collection of Jeff Kerns, Los Angeles, CA / Photo Credit: Gene Ogami

46 Family photo
Courtesy of the artist

47 Family photo
Courtesy of the artist

48 Family photo
Courtesy of the artist

49 Family photo
Courtesy of the artist

50 *Car 23*
2008
1964 Toyota Land Cruiser, oil paint, stickers
73" x 154" x 80"
Courtesy of the artist

51 *Rocinante* (Installation view)
COLA 2010 at the Los Angeles Municipal Art Gallery, Barnsdall Art Park, Los Angeles, CA, May 20–July 18, 2010
1979 Mazda RX-7, wood, nylon strap, music box playing "Windmills of your Mind"
52" x 42" x 33"
Courtesy of Susanne Vielmetter Los Angeles Projects / Photo Credit: Gene Ogami

Mastodon (Installation view)
COLA 2010 at the Los Angeles Municipal Art Gallery, Barnsdall Art Park, Los Angeles, CA, May 20–July 18, 2010
1979 Mazda RX-7, wood, nylon strap, music box playing "Windmills of your Mind"
82" x 31" x 36"
Courtesy of Susanne Vielmetter Los Angeles Projects / Photo Credit: Gene Ogami

52 *Sean Duffy: Hilites* (Installation view)
Miami Art Museum, New Work Gallery, July 18–October 12, 2008
Courtesy of the Miami Art Museum, Miami, FL / Photo Credit: Nancy Watson

53 *Individual Record: "Boombox"*
2006
archival inkjet print in clear plastic sleeve
12" x 12"
Courtesy of the artist

54 *Almost in Love*
2010
two turntables, speakers
Courtesy of the Laguna Art Museum, Laguna Beach, CA / Photo Credit: Robert Wedemeyer

55 *Spider and the Fly* (Detail view)
2006
turntable, mixer, two speakers, The Rolling Stones "Satisfaction" and "The Spider and the Fly" singles, seven albums of various artist covers of "Satisfaction" and "The Spider and the Fly"
6.5" x 17" x 15" turntable, 13.5" x 23" x 7.5" mixer, 11" x 15.5" x 7" speakers
Courtesy of SUSANNE VIELMETTER LOS ANGELES PROJECTS / Photo Credit: GENE OGAMI

56 *Kraftwerk*
2004
three 2055 Kenwood turntables, mixer, speakers, Kraftwerk record albums
Dimensions variable, 6" x 19" x 31" turntable
Courtesy of SUSANNE VIELMETTER LOS ANGELES PROJECTS / Collection of WILHELM SCHUERMAN, AACHEN, GERMANY / Photo Credit: GENE OGAMI

57 *Individual Record: "My Life Time Studio Assistant"*
2006
archival inkjet print in clear plastic sleeve
7" x 7"
Courtesy of the artist

58 *Individual Record: "The Original Sound"*
2006
archival inkjet print in clear plastic sleeve
12" x 12"
Courtesy of the artist

59 *Individual Record: "Group Show 2"*
2007
archival inkjet print in clear plastic sleeve
12" x 12"
Courtesy of the artist

60 *Individual Record: "Scares"*
2007
archival inkjet print in clear plastic sleeve
7" x 7"
Courtesy of the artist

61 *Burn-Out Sun*
2003
20 LPs, metal tripod, glue
42" x 33" x 33"
Courtesy of SUSANNE VIELMETTER LOS ANGELES PROJECTS / Collection of DENNIS AND DEBRA SCHOLL, MIAMI BEACH, FL / Photo Credit: GENE OGAMI

62 *Individual Record: "It's Burnt Out Sun Time! ...again!!!"*
2007
archival inkjet print in clear plastic sleeve
12" x 12"
Courtesy of the artist

Q & A

A *Rerecorder*
2002
two cassette recorders, cardboard box, wood, tapes
4" x 6" x 15"
Courtesy of SUSANNE VIELMETTER LOS ANGELES PROJECTS / Collection of CARLOS MOTA, NEW YORK, NY

Book Insert

Individual Record: "Sean Duffy and the Front Forty Press"
2011
4/4 offset book insert
4" x 4"
Courtesy of the artist

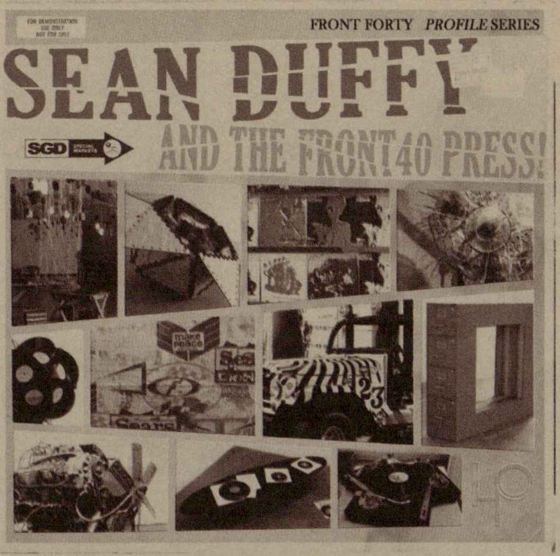

LISTEN TO THE *spectacular* SOUNDS OF *Sean Duffy!*

To hear audio from some of the pieces you have seen in this book please visit the Front Forty Press website. Use the link and password provided below. Enjoy!

http://front40press.com/seanduffy

PASSWORD: tonearm